LITERARY LODGINGS

Elaine Borish

LITERARY LODGINGS

Constable · London

First published in Great Britain 1984
by Constable and Company Limited
10 Orange Street, London WC2H 7EG
Copyright © 1984 by Elaine Borish
ISBN 0 09 465180 9
Set in Linotron Plantin 11pt
by Rowland Phototypesetting Limited
Bury St Edmunds, Suffolk
Printed in Great Britain
by St Edmundsbury Press
Bury St Edmunds, Suffolk

To the wonderful person who shared the work
and the fun in the making of this book –
to my husband

ACKNOWLEDGEMENTS

The Publishers would like to acknowledge the following sources from which short quotations have been taken: Noël Coward, *Present Indicative* (Heinemann, 1974) and *Private Lives* (Samuel French, 1948); E M Forster, *A Room with a View* (Edward Arnold, 1908); A E Housman, *Collected Poems* (Cape, 1960); Rudyard Kipling *Verse* (definitive edition, Hodder & Stoughton, 1940), and *Actions and Reactions* (Macmillan, 1909); Beatrix Potter, *Tale of Pigling Bland* (Warne, 1913) and *Journal of Beatrix Potter 1881–93* edited by Leslie Linder (Warne, 1966); Dylan Thomas, *Letters to Vernon Watkins* (Greenwood Press, 1982), and *Poems* edited by Daniel Jones (Dent, 1974); Evelyn Waugh, *Diaries* edited by Michael Davie (Weidenfeld & Nicolson, 1976), and *Letters* edited by Mark Amory (Weidenfeld & Nicolson, 1980); Edith Wharton 'Terminus' (1909 copyright © William R. Tyler); Virginia Woolf, *To the Lighthouse* (Hogarth Press, 1929); *Mrs Dalloway* (Hogarth Press, 1925); *Diaries, volume 3* edited by A. O. Bell (Hogarth Press, 1980) and *Letters, volume 1* edited by N Nicolson and J Trautmann (Hogarth Press, 1975)

E.B.
1984

CONTENTS

CONTENTS

CONTENTS

SCOTLAND

[ix]

ILLUSTRATIONS

Note The following portraits are published by kind permission of the National Portrait Gallery, London: Arnold Bennett, Oscar Wilde, Rudyard Kipling, John Keats, Edward Lear, Alfred Lord Tennyson, Virginia Woolf, Benjamin Disraeli, Lewis Carroll, A. E. Housman, Noël Coward, Charles Dickens and Beatrix Potter. The portrait of Edith Wharton is published by courtesy of Gessford, N.Y.

INTRODUCTION

People have always been fascinated with places associated with authors, and the literary pilgrimage has long been accepted as a good excuse for travel. What better way to worship at the shrine of a beloved or respected author than to visit the actual location which was once part of the writer's life and is perhaps reflected in the books?

A journey to the haunts of a favourite author can only deepen love and understanding and result in a thrilling emotional experience. Seeing the plaque that marks the house in which Charles Dickens was born, the landscape that inspired Wordsworth, or the writing-box used by Jane Austen—all of these give great pleasure and satisfaction to untold numbers.

But how these delights increase when the traveller is able to *stay* in the place where a favourite author once lived! When the traveller can dine and lodge in the very house in which the author once dined and lodged and acquire an intimacy not otherwise available, what ineffable joy may result!

Fortunately, writers also travelled and often wrote their immortal lines in inns or lodgings that continue to excite, sometimes only because of the literary connection. Or perhaps the home in which the writer once lived changed hands over the years to become a hotel. As a hotel guest, the literary pilgrim is able to revel in the author's own past surroundings.

Unfortunately, writers did not always oblige by selecting in their travels places destined to remain intact for future generations. They may have stayed in inns which have fallen victim to the ravages of time, or they may have stayed with friends, or taken furnished rooms to frustrate devoted followers.

Sometimes the hotel in question may have reverted to a private house—like the Lob's Wood Hotel in Surrey which was

[xv]

once the home of J. M. Barrie, its magical woods and nearby lake his Never-Never Land. Or like the King's Arms in Kenilworth where Sir Walter Scott stayed while collecting material for his novel, *Kenilworth*, but which recently ceased to offer lodgings and now functions merely as a pub.

Only buildings that once housed writers and exist today as hotels are included in this book. The rule for *Literary Lodgings* is that the hotel in Britain associated with an author must be alive, the author not.

Because the presence of some former clients will nourish the prestige of hotels, hotels take pride in the association. Often they are so eager to be identified with a celebrity that they make inaccurate claims with a 'Queen Elizabeth slept here' syndrome. Worse yet, they make research more difficult.

Although Jane Austen never journeyed north of the Trent, a charming little inn in Derbyshire boasts of her presence there. Simply because they are located on a river, several hotels elect Izaak Walton as a former guest. Claims for Dr Johnson and Charlotte Brontë are difficult to substantiate. And so it goes on.

The visitor approaching the stately historic house of an author, or envisioning a grand architectural façade with columned portico and steps flanked by royal beasts, may well wonder precisely what lines were written between the lions. Even when the building under consideration is a country cottage or a big city hotel, questions arise: What were the circumstances which brought the writer to this place? When? How was he influenced by it? What did he write there? What are the relevant facts in the particular period of the author's life? What is the hotel like today? Is it worth a visit?

Here is an invitation to pleasurable holidays. Satisfaction awaits the follower who adopts the words of the Biblical Ruth: for whither thou goest, I will go; and where thou lodgest, I will lodge.

LONDON AND THE SOUTH-EAST

★ ★ ★

ARNOLD BENNETT

★ ★ ★

at

THE SAVOY
STRAND
LONDON WC2

In the façade a few windows burned here and
there, somehow mournfully. He knew the
exact number of guests staying in the hotel
that night; but their secrets, misfortunes,
anxieties, hopes, despairs, tragedies, he did
not know. And he would have liked to know
every one of them.

Imperial Palace

In a corner of North Staffordshire, in the valley of the River
Trent, lies a chain of six towns called 'the Potteries': Tunstall,
Burslem, Hanley, Stoke-upon-Trent, Fenton and Longton.
This industrial conglomeration, the only region in England
named for the work that is done there, was incorporated in
1910 as the city of Stoke-on-Trent and known familiarly as
Stoke. Bottle-shaped kilns once blackened the area as they did
their coal firing to produce pottery and porcelain known by
such names as Wedgwood, Spode, Royal Doulton and
Copeland.

Enoch Arnold Bennett first saw the smoke of Stoke from
Hanley where he was born, on 27 May 1867, the eldest of six
children. But he is associated with a house in Waterloo Road
(Trafalgar Road in his novels) in Burslem (Bursley) in which
he grew up. At twenty-one he managed to escape from the
restrictions of his provincial life and from his father's

autocratic rule by obtaining work in London as a shorthand clerk for a firm of solicitors.

He dabbled in freelance journalism and won a writing competition which encouraged him to consider a change in career. He left the law firm in 1894 and went to work for *Woman* writing articles and reviews. A few years later, he became assistant editor and then editor of that weekly magazine, and at thirty-one he was ready to try to earn his living by writing fiction.

His first novel, *A Man from the North* (1890), is about a man who comes to London from the Potteries, works in a lawyer's office, writes articles and tries to produce a novel. The auto-biographical elements are recognisable but, unlike his fictional hero who failed in his ambition to become a writer, Arnold Bennett became an author upon publication of this book.

Success came with his discovery that he could use the familiar background of his youth for fiction. *Anna of the Five Towns* was his first novel set in the Potteries. He recreated the region he knew, giving artistic order to the shapeless sprawl of towns. He made six equal five by eliminating Fenton and calling the area the Five Towns, a name that has caught on in a world he has immortalised. He captured the essence of life in the Potteries in such collections of short stories as *The Grim Smile of the Five Towns* and *The Matador of the Five Towns* and in such novels as *The Card*, *The Old Wives' Tale* and the Clayhanger trilogy (*Clayhanger*, *Hilda Lessways* and *These Twain*).

He also captured success as a novelist. A hard worker, he knew how to live well with the money he earned. After he had finished writing his first novel, he made his first trip abroad, to Belgium. He loved foreign travel and made a visit to Paris the following year. In later years, he fulfilled his dream of owning a yacht.

Paris had enormous appeal for him and, at the age of thirty-five, after publication of *Anna of the Five Towns*, he decided to live in the capital of modern realism. In Paris, in 1907, he

Arnold Bennett (1867–1931) and the Thames Foyer of The Savoy Hotel, London, on which he based his novel *Imperial Palace*

married a Frenchwoman, Marguerite Soulié. He continued to plunge himself into his work, and the books he produced include *The Old Wives' Tale,* regarded as his masterpiece. When he returned to settle in England, where he bought a country house in Essex in 1913, his reputation was made.

These Twain (1916) was the last of the Potteries novels. He became active in the London theatre and wrote plays, sometimes in collaboration, and he wrote stage adaptations of his own works. He gradually spent more and more time in London, occasionally staying at the Savoy, and eventually he left his country house. With a flat in London, he made the city his home as well as his subject.

Shortly after his marriage ended in 1921 by a deed of separation, he met and fell in love with Dorothy Cheston, an extremely attractive actress who was appearing in the Liverpool production of his play, *Body and Soul.* Marguerite refused to grant a divorce, but he was to spend his remaining years with Dorothy. His first and only child, a daughter, was born in 1926.

Despite his love for travel, Bennett was not a wise traveller. On his last visit to France, in December 1930, he drank tap water in his room and was reproached by Dorothy. In their Paris hotel restaurant, he drank carafe water and was reproached by the waiter. Back in London he forced himself to work on *Dream of Destiny* although he was feeling unwell. In February his illness was diagnosed as typhoid. As his condition grew worse and he lay ill in a semi-conscious or semi-delirious state, straw was spread on the busy streets outside his flat over Baker Street station to diminish the noise of the traffic. The life of the man from the north ended on 26 March 1931.

Tributes flowed in from the anxious world which had watched. Even Virginia Woolf, who attacked him in *Mr Bennett and Mrs Brown* for being preoccupied with externals, wrote these moving words in her diary: 'Arnold Bennett died last night, which leaves me sadder than I should have supposed. A lovable genuine man . . . Some real understanding power, as well as gigantic absorbing power. Queer how one

[4]

regrets the dispersal of anybody who seemed—as I say—genuine: who had direct contact with life—for he abused me; and yet I rather wished him to go on abusing me; and me abusing him.'

He was a generous and beloved person. Somerset Maugham said, 'It was impossible to know him without liking him.' H. G. Wells wrote that he 'radiated and evoked affection to an unusual degree.' Rebecca West declared, 'London will not seem quite London without his flamboyant figure.'

As a novelist he is well remembered, not only as a regional writer of the Potteries, but as a writer who could turn his pen to any subject. Two of his finest later novels take place in London—*Riceyman Steps* (1923) and *Imperial Palace* (1930).

Imperial Palace, his last and longest novel, immortalises the Savoy in its detailed study of every aspect of the running of a great hotel. Bennett placed his fictional hotel next to St James's Park rather than in the Strand alongside the Thames, and he always maintained that it was not the Savoy. Nevertheless, the Imperial Palace is indistinguishable from the Savoy.

Perhaps because of his own deprived and provincial background, perhaps because of his addiction to travel, Bennett was fascinated by hotels. He had used the luxury hotel theme in an early novel, *The Grand Babylon Hotel* (1902), and references to hotels appear throughout his novels. A character exclaims in *Hilda Lessways*, 'Hotels! There'll be more money and more fun to be got out of Hotels soon than of any other kind of enterprise in the world!'

Bennett felt compelled to return to the intriguing subject in his final work. He wrote in his journal on 25 September 1929: 'The big *hotel de luxe* is a very serious organisation; it is in my opinion a unique subject for a serious novel; it is stuffed with human nature of extremely various kinds. The subject is characteristic of the age; it is as modern as the morning's milk; it is tremendous, and worthy of tremendous handling. I dare say it's beyond me.'

[5]

In preparation for the novel he had lunch, in March 1927, with the publicity director of the Savoy who gave him an abundance of ideas. He had frequent meetings with managing director, George Reeves-Smith, to whom he dedicated his novel, 'from one of the warmest of his admirers'. The original manuscript is now among the hotel's private treasures.

Bennett stayed at the Savoy while accumulating the facts and minute details on the organisation and running of a gigantic luxury hotel, the finest in the world. The officials co-operated with him in every way. In a letter of 15 September 1929 from the Savoy to his nephew he wrote: 'I am now staying here. I am collecting hotel-material for my novel, and I never had such material . . . Hard work collecting it; but everything is open to me and everybody at my disposition. I visited the laundry the other day . . .'

Bennett takes the reader into laundries and kitchens and cellars. He calls one chapter 'Bowels of the Hotel'. We are given this view of the kitchens: 'The kitchens of the Imperial Palace restaurant were on the same floor as the restaurant itself, and immediately adjoining it. You passed through an open door, hidden like a guilty secret from all the dining-tables, then up a very short corridor, and at one step you were in another and a different world: a super-heated world of steel glistening and dull, and bare wood, and food in mass raw and cooked, and bustle, and hurrying to and fro, and running to and fro, and calling and even raucous shouting in French and Italian: a world of frenzied industry . . .'

With such outpouring of the details of hotel business, the reader is prepared to be bored. He is not. The details go on and on, but interest rarely wanes as Bennett takes us behind the scenes and through the keyholes.

Out of a cast of eighty-five, there are three central characters: Evelyn Orcham, the talented managing director who has made the Imperial Palace first among luxury hotels of the world; Violet Powler, who rises from a post in the laundry to head housekeeper; and Gracie Savott, wealthy daughter of millionaire financier, Sir Henry Savott, who

[6]

schemes to negotiate a merger of the hotel. But the character of the hotel is central to the novel.

As·for the plot, with a quarter of a million words in the novel, the action could be summarised in about a dozen: It is about the proposed merger by which Savott gets control of the 'unique hotel'. But Bennett communicates his fascination as he presents a study of humanity in the milieu of a hotel.

But what a hotel! The history of the Savoy begins in 1246 when Henry III presented to Queen Eleanor's Uncle Peter, Count of Savoy, a parcel of land between London and Westminster on which he built a splendid palace. It was eventually destroyed but the site was destined to contain, some six hundred and fifty years later, another kind of dazzling palace—a great luxury hotel called the Savoy. A gilt statue of Count Peter now has a prominent position over the span in the Strand courtyard entrance to the Savoy.

In the forecourt of the hotel is the famous Savoy Theatre, associated with Richard D'Oyly Carte, the impresario who inspired the Gilbert and Sullivan partnership and built the new Savoy Theatre as a home for their highly successful operettas. The Savoy Theatre, the first in the world to have electric lights, opened with *Patience* in October 1881. To keep the theatre entrance free from the clutter of waiting vehicles, the forecourt exists as the only thoroughfare in England in which traffic keeps to the right.

Richard D'Oyly Carte saw the advantage of having a fashionable hotel adjacent to his theatre and, in his role as hotelier, he began the construction of a hotel in 1884. Five years later, the seven-storey, steel-framed building, which used concrete for the first time, was completed. Though only half the size it is now, perhaps its most startling feature was the existence of a huge number of bathrooms—seventy. (A recently-opened rival hotel boasted four bathrooms for its five hundred guests.)

The Savoy was the epitome of luxury. D'Oyly Carte secured the services of the best available people in the world to look after the cuisine and management—Auguste Escoffier and

César Ritz. The hotel glittered with royalty and with society personalities. The legend had begun; the legend continues, even as the hotel approaches its centenary.

Step through the revolving doors and you are in a jewelled city. The large pillared lobby with reception and service areas offers choices that lead to the famous Grill Room, or to the American Bar and Shopping Arcade, to the Drawing Room or lifts. Or straight ahead to the sumptuously-decorated Thames foyer with white piano contained within a gazebo—a divine setting for afternoon tea with musical accompaniment—and beyond it is the River Restaurant with a glorious view across the Thames.

Equally and predictably luxurious are the two hundred guest rooms with their individual and antique furnishings. Suites consisting of bedroom and sitting room overlook the River Thames which adds a breathtaking view to impeccable service.

Always attentive to pleasing guests, the hotel has even made culinary history. Once, after a theatrical first night, the chef of the Savoy created for Arnold Bennett, a recherché dish known as Omelette Arnold Bennett, a large open omelette made with smoked haddock. So the well-known and well-liked novelist, one of the few non-opera singers to be commemorated by a special dish, is well-remembered at the Savoy; his name may be sought on the menu between the soufflé Tetrazzini and Pêche Melba (which also had their debuts here). And the distinguished Savoy, in turn, has the distinction of being the setting and subject of a novel by an equally distinguished author.

OSCAR WILDE

at

THE CADOGAN HOTEL
SLOANE STREET
LONDON SWI

Each narrow cell in which we dwell
Is a foul and dark latrine,
And the fetid breath of living Death
Chokes up each grated screen,
And all, but Lust, is turned to Dust
In Humanity's machine.

The Ballad of Reading Gaol

A negative literary tour of England might include the London street where Dryden was beaten up and left for dead, or the River Ouse where Virginia Woolf drowned herself, or the church of Framlingham in Suffolk where the poet Surrey lies buried having been beheaded after conviction on a charge of high treason, or the site of the jail in Bedford where John Bunyan was incarcerated. It could also include the Cadogan Hotel in London where Oscar Wilde was arrested.

The events leading to Oscar Wilde's popularity and fame as a writer are less complicated than the events leading to his arrest and imprisonment. From his prison cell in Reading Gaol he wrote, 'The two great turning-points in my life were when my father sent me to Oxford, and when society sent me to prison.'

The starting point of his life was 16 October 1854 in Dublin, where Oscar Fingal O'Flahertie Wills Wilde was born to parents with strong literary tastes which both he and his elder brother Willie inherited. He went to Trinity College, Dublin. Then came Magdalen College, Oxford. After the long university career he came to London, in 1879.

In London he made a charming host noted for his witty

[9]

sayings. He became famous as an epigrammatist and raconteur as well as an author of poems, fiction, and plays. In 1881, his book of poems was privately printed. In that year also he tried to secure the production of his play *Vera*. He was to write other unsuccessful plays before his career as a playwright was established with *Lady Windermere's Fan* in 1892, followed by *Salome, A Woman of No Importance, An Ideal Husband, The Importance of Being Earnest*.

But he was lifted out of obscurity and thrust into the limelight by an accident, by Gilbert and Sullivan's *Patience* of 1881, which satirised the so-called aesthetic or pre-Raphaelite movement. Wilde was invited to America to give a lecture in January 1882, prior to the New York production, in a publicity scheme to show the public what the movement was all about and thereby increase interest in the operetta. It increased interest in him. People came to believe that the character of Reginald Bunthorne, the fleshly poet who walked down Piccadilly with a poppy or a lily in his medieval hand, was based on Wilde; and Wilde capitalised on that impression. 'Anyone could have done that,' he said. 'The great and difficult thing was what I achieved—to make the whole world believe that I had done it.'

Back from his successful American tour early in 1883, Wilde renewed his friendship with Constance Lloyd, whom he married the following year. He had a reasonably happy marriage and was on the threshold of a brilliant career.

He edited *Woman's World* from 1887 and became a writer of note, with many clever short stories and with the novel *The Picture of Dorian Gray* to his credit. He seemed to be fulfilling the prediction written in his own words, in the year of his graduation from Oxford: 'I'll be a poet, a writer, a dramatist. Somehow or other I'll be famous, and if not famous, I'll be notorious.'

The year 1891 represents a peak in his literary career with his acceptance everywhere as a fine talent. But that was also a fateful year, for in 1891 he met Lord Alfred Douglas—'Bosie'—and the meeting led to the catastrophe of his life. Wilde, an established author and famous society personality, a married

Oscar Wilde (1854–1900)
and The Cadogan (Thistle)
Hotel, London, where he
was arrested

man with two children, was thirty-six when he was introduced to the twenty-year-old Oxford undergraduate with a flair for poetry. The love affair which was to develop between them led, inexorably, to Wilde's downfall.

Douglas was the third son of the eighth Marquis of Queensberry, the instigator of the Queensberry Rules of Boxing. The eccentric nobleman, vain, tyrannical and subject to fits of fury, had abused his wife, neglected his family, and ignored his son's existence. Now he became aroused by the liaison between the two and launched a series of threats and attacks culminating in a message which he left for Wilde at his club. On the back of a visiting card were the words with the famous misspelling, 'For Oscar Wilde posing as somdomite.'

Wilde brought action for libel against the Marquis of Queensberry, assuring his solicitor that he was innocent of the charge. When Queensberry's counsel threatened to produce a number of youths to testify with incriminating evidence, Wilde's counsel decided to withdraw from the prosecution, and Queensberry was found not guilty.

Having been made to appear guilty by facts and information which came out as a result of the examination, Wilde was now liable to prosecution for offences. He was, after all, living outside the law, albeit an unjust or even a cruel law. Queensberry's agents rounded up witnesses by bribing them, or threatening them with prosecution and prison, and produced a collection of disreputable people with whom Wilde was alleged to have associated. With things stacked against him by such unscrupulous means, Wilde should have abandoned the action and gone abroad. By proceeding with it, he was doomed.

After the verdict, he was urged by friends to take the boat train across the Channel, but he went instead to the Cadogan Hotel. He did not flee but was overtaken by inertia or some inexplicable need to be a martyr. There he stayed, drinking and waiting for the inevitable to happen. A warrant of arrest was issued on 5 April 1895 at about five o'clock, and a few hours later came the fatal knock on his door.

[12]

After the trial, the judge summarised Wilde as 'the centre of a circle of extensive corruption of the most hideous kind among young men.' (More hideous than murder, one wonders.) He was given the maximum sentence possible, of imprisonment for two years with hard labour. He was forty-one and to all intents and purposes, his life was over.

A character in *Lady Windermere's Fan* says, 'Misfortunes one can endure—they come from outside, they are accidents. But to suffer for one's own faults—ah!—there is the sting of life.' Wilde knew he brought his troubles on himself.

Prison conditions were harsh and inhumane, and his suffering and humiliation were increased by his being made a bankrupt by the vindictive Queensberry and by having his children legally taken from him. Released on 19 May 1897, he left for France.

An injury to the middle ear received in prison from a fall in his cell caused him continuous discomfort and pain. He submitted to surgery but never fully recovered from the operation, which was performed in October 1900. He contracted cerebral meningitis and died in Paris on 30 November, six weeks after his forty-sixth birthday.

The Cadogan Hotel maintains the room which was his, the very lovely Room 118 with crystal chandelier, blue draperies over the windows and pink padded headboard over the bed. The curved window seat in the corner alcove overlooking Sloane Street and Cadogan Place is a comfortable spot for viewing the pretty London scene outside and for reviewing the tragic scene which took place inside. But in such a bright and cheerful environment, it is difficult to visualise the dark events:

Wilde, his face expressionless, is seated in an armchair by the fireplace smoking. His friends are seated at a table on which are half-empty glasses of hock. Arresting officers arrive and read out the charge of 'committing acts of gross indecency with various male persons'. Wilde leaves with the Scotland Yard detectives.

Fortunately, the Cadogan Hotel itself yields a positive

report. The five-storey, red-brick Victorian building, located in fashionable Chelsea, is not much changed from the time it was built in the late nineteenth century.

The peaceful and elegant atmosphere which characterises the entire ground floor begins in the small entrance area with panelled walls, oak reception desk and porter's desk, and old-fashioned cage lift next to the carpeted stairway. Ersatz Grinling Gibbons wood carvings of lions, floral garlands and bunches of fruit on the desks, pillars, and walls add interest to the decor as well as a touch of history. The lions are from the crest of Lord Cadogan.

Beyond the reception area, a cedar-panelled lounge is decorated in warm colours with comfortable settees and armchairs, a very friendly and inviting room. Beyond is the bar with an elaborate plaster ceiling, and through arches can be seen the impressively elegant dining room. On the walls of the bar are photographs of Oscar Wilde as well as Lillie Langtry—a reminder that the back half of the hotel was formerly her private residence. A restored Lillie Langtry Room represents a part of her home just as it was when she entertained such notables as the artist James McNeill Whistler and Oscar Wilde. Now used for conferences, it displays the deeds of transfer of her house to the hotel. All is successfully designed to give a peaceful turn-of-the century feeling.

The feeling of contentment carries over to thoughts of Oscar Wilde. Here he can be remembered for the legacy of laughter and comedy which he left. He defies his own aphorism that 'one can survive everything nowadays except death.' The last word was his. Biographies, films, and plays continue to be written on his life and work; his plays are continually being performed, and his writing remains in print. His epigrams have become part of the language: 'I can resist everything except temptation.'

His best aphorisms are a mixture of fun and profundity: 'Experience is the name all men give to their mistakes.' Although axioms taken from his comedies are meant to be played for laughs, they also have serious application to life. A character in *Lady Windermere's Fan* says, 'In this world there are only two tragedies. One is not getting what one wants and the other is getting it.' Wilde wrote in *A Woman of No Importance,* 'The only difference between the saint and the sinner is that every saint has a past, and every sinner has a future.' Perhaps it can be said that Oscar Wilde had both.

When the master of the instant riposte was asked by an American customs officer whether he had anything to declare, he replied, 'Nothing. Nothing but my genius!' Indeed, his genius survives in the works he created which continue to amuse and entertain.

Rudyard Kipling

at

BROWN'S HOTEL
DOVER STREET
LONDON W I

At the bottom of the valley a little brook had
undermined its footbridge, and frothed in the
wreckage. But there stood great woods on the
slopes beyond—old, tall, and brilliant, like
unfaded tapestries against the walls of a ruined
house.
'All this within a hundred miles of
London,' he said.

An Habitation Enforced

Brown's Hotel is still the place one goes to for elegant old
world atmosphere. In the pleasant surroundings of the
lounge, tea at four o'clock is a most agreeable and traditional
institution.

Throughout the hotel there are oak-panelled walls hung
with prints and paintings. Fireplaces, carpeting, and warm-
coloured fabrics contribute to the style and unhurried scene.
The hotel has 165 bedrooms furnished and decorated traditionally, each room with character of its own.

From its inception in 1837, the year when Queen Victoria
began her reign, Brown's Hotel has shown concern for the
care and comfort of clients. James Brown opened his hotel at
23 Dover Street in the select residential district of Mayfair. He
was able gradually to expand his successful venture by acquir-
ing three neighbouring houses, numbers 22, 24 and 21. The
four buildings together make up the Dover Street front as
seen today.

Mr and Mrs Brown knew how to cater to the needs of the

Rudyard Kipling
(1865–1936) and
Brown's Hotel, Dover
St, London, where he
spent his honeymoon

gentry. The proprietor's wife had been lady's maid to Lady Byron, and that connection with the poet's family is recalled by the present Byron Room.

The hotel was sold to James John Ford in 1859 and taken over by his son Henry, who managed the hotel for forty-six years beginning in 1882. Improvements continued to take place. Electric lighting came in 1884 followed by 'fixed baths' in the following year. An expansion programme in the late 1880s extended the hotel at the back to Albemarle Street. Finally, it was acquired by Trusthouse Forte in 1948. But the hotel has kept the original and simple name as well as the standards and traditions set in Brown's day.

From country gentry and wealthy American tourists to royalty—in fact and in fiction—Brown's Hotel in Mayfair was *the* place. Characters in a novel by Edith Wharton regularly alighted at Brown's, as did characters from real life such as Henry James. In more recent times, Agatha Christie used it as the setting for *At Bertram's Hotel*. A sampling from the list of visitors is impressive.

Alexander Graham Bell came in 1876 carrying his invention which, he explained to the owner's young son, could carry voices along wires. On the ground floor next to the Byron Room is the Graham Bell Room, from which the first telephone call in Britain was made. Theodore Roosevelt came in 1886, taking time out to marry Edith Kermit Carew; a copy of the marriage certificate hangs in the hotel. Upstairs, the Roosevelt Room contains a portrait of the twenty-sixth President of the United States. Mark Twain slept here. And an American honeymoon couple, Franklin and Eleanor Roosevelt, stayed in 1905. In what is now the Hellenic Suite, the exiled King George of Greece held court from 1924 until the monarchy was restored in 1935. And during World War II, the Dutch government in exile declared war on Japan in Room 36 of Brown's Hotel.

One attractive room, decorated with illustrations from the works of Kipling and with his portrait over the mantelpiece, is named after the literary celebrity. The Kipling Room is part of the suite that Kipling always occupied during his frequent visits to the hotel.

Rudyard Kipling was himself named for the place in England where his parents became engaged—the delightful village of Rudyard in Staffordshire on the edge of the Peak District National Park. The young married couple left England to live in India, where John Lockwood Kipling had secured a teaching position at the Fine Arts School in Bombay. Later that year, their first child, Rudyard, was born in Bombay on 30 December 1865.

It was normal practice for Anglo-Indian children to be sent home to England to be educated in the healthier climate of a country not ravaged by dangerous epidemic diseases. Thus, when Rudyard was six and his sister Alice three, the children were placed with an English family in Southsea on the Hampshire coast. Unfortunately, they were mistreated and miserable. Mrs Holloway, or 'Aunty Rosa' as she was called, apparently disliked Ruddy and subjected him to unkind treatment and frequent beatings. Only after five unhappy years in that foster home did his mother discover the horrendous conditions and extricate Rudyard from the hateful environment. He was then sent to school, to the United Services College, in a resort town in Devon named Westward Ho! after the title of the popular novel by Charles Kingsley. The picture of odious school life was brilliantly told in a later work of fiction, *Stalky & Co*. The preface poem of that novel includes these stanzas:

> Western wind and open surge
>   Took us from our mothers;
> Flung us on a naked shore
> (Twelve bleak houses by the shore!
> Seven summers by the shore!)
>   'Mid two hundred brothers.
>
> There we met with famous men
>   Set in office o'er us;

> And they beat on us with rods—
> Faithfully with many rods—
> Daily beat on us with rods,
>   For the love they bore us.

But Rudyard left the school after five summers, not seven as stated in the poem. Unsuited to a military career for which the school prepared its inmates, he sailed for India in September 1882.

His career as a writer flowered in Lahore where he was given his first employment as a journalist on the local newspaper. His father had taken up a new post as curator of the museum in Lahore, and Rudyard, not yet seventeen, was able to live happily with his family while reporting for the *Civil and Military Gazette*. The Indian stories he later wrote were to bring him immense fame, but he left India for good in 1889 and never returned except for a very short visit to his parents in 1891.

London was the place for making a literary reputation, and to London he went. He settled in Villiers Street and wrote. From those cheap lodgings in Charing Cross, the struggling writer became the successful author who frequented Brown's Hotel.

Kipling met an American literary agent and publisher, Wolcott Balestier. The relationship flourished and developed into a deep and intimate friendship. The two men even collaborated on the writing of a novel.

Kipling's two successful years in London brought him critical acclaim. Feeling the strain of overwork, he embarked in August on a recuperative journey which took him to South Africa, New Zealand, Australia, Ceylon and India. In Lahore, in December 1891, Kipling received word of the sudden death by typhoid of his dear friend. Distraught, Kipling returned to London and immediately announced his intention of marrying Wolcott's elder sister Caroline. It seemed to many that mutual love for the dead man was the only thing they had in common.

Henry James attended the wedding on 18 January 1892, perhaps reluctantly, for he wrote to his brother William that Carrie seemed 'a hard, devoted, capable little person, whom I don't in the least understand his marrying. It's a union of which I don't forecast the future though I gave her away at the altar in a dreary little wedding.' Nevertheless, it was a happy marriage, full of love and care and understanding.

The honeymoon night and wedding breakfast were set in Brown's Hotel. When the young couple left on the 26th, their hotel bill for £22 was presented, paid in full, by the owner as a wedding gift. To Brown's Hotel, Rudyard Kipling returned continually throughout life.

The Kiplings lived in Vermont, Carrie's American home, for the first four years of their marriage. But on holidays to England from Vermont, they stayed at Brown's. On finally leaving America and returning to England in 1895, they stayed with his parents in Tisbury and then in Rottingdean, but expeditions to London were set at Brown's Hotel. They partook of the London literary and social scene, and Brown's continued to be an essential way of life for the Kiplings even after they moved into their permanent home in the country.

In 1902 Kipling found the dream house—Bateman's—in which he lived for the rest of his life. The grey stone house with the date AD 1634 inscribed over the door, with its oak beams and staircase, has become a National Trust property and is open to the public. Its remote location in the small village of Burwash in East Sussex, some fifty miles from London, gave Kipling the privacy he longed for. He settled in, as did the American couple who settle in England in *An Habitation Enforced*. The poem which follows that short story, *The Recall*, begins with these two verses:

> I am the land of their fathers,
> In me the virtue stays.
> I will bring back my children
> After certain days.

> Under their feet in the grasses
> My clinging magic runs.
> They shall return as strangers,
> They shall remain as sons.

Kipling found roots in the Sussex countryside, which became new subject matter for his writing. He used the surroundings of Bateman's for such volumes as *Puck of Pook's Hill* and *Rewards and Fairies*.

But escape from the country was also necessary, and he escaped, inevitably, to Brown's. It was the place for deep emotional scenes and key events. The Kiplings spent most of the war years at the hotel, and he saw visitors there as well as at Bateman's. In those terrible war years he was to lose the second of his three children. Earlier, in 1899, their beloved daughter Josephine had died at the age of seven while the family were on a visit in New York. Now, his son John was reported missing in action. One visitor to Brown's at that time was his old friend Julia Catlin. When he escorted her to her car, Kipling said, 'Down on your knees, Julia, and thank God you haven't a son.' His son John died in the battle of Loos in October 1915, and the body was never recovered.

> 'Have you news of my boy Jack?'
> *Not this tide.*
> 'When d'you think that he'll come back?'
> *Not with this wind blowing, and this tide.*
>
> 'Has any one else had word of him?'
> *Not this tide.*
> *For what is sunk will hardly swim,*
> *Not with this wind blowing, and this tide.*

He did much writing at the hotel and dictated an account of Canadian troops landing in Flanders. His cousin and friend Stanley Baldwin visited and wrote of breakfast with Kipling and a pleasant time at the hotel.

Indeed, Kipling spent so much time there that he was asked why they did not have their own place in London after the war instead of always being at Brown's. His answer, a reference to Carrie's compulsiveness as a housewife, was, 'Mother couldn't run two houses.'

A month after his seventieth birthday, while at Brown's Hotel, he had a violent haemorrhage and was rushed to Middlesex Hospital where he died four days later, on 17 January 1936.

EDITH WHARTON

at

THE CHARING CROSS HOTEL
STRAND
LONDON WC2

And the low wide bed, as rutted and worn as a high-road,
The bed with its soot sodden chintz, the grime of its brasses,
That has born the weight of fagged bodies, dust-stained,
        averted in sleep,
The hurried, the restless, the aimless—

Terminus

'I think the full tide of human existence is at Charing Cross,'
Dr Johnson remarked long before a great mainline railway
and underground station with a vast railway hotel also marked
the site. The name of Charing Cross derives from the stone
cross, the last of twelve set up by a heartbroken Edward I in
1290 to mark the resting places of his beloved Queen Eleanor
as her funeral cortege travelled slowly from Harby in Notting-
hamshire where she died to Westminster Abbey where she
was buried. A parliamentary decree of 1643 destroyed the
monument, and it is actually an 1863 replica of the original
cross that stands in the forecourt before the great Charing
Cross Hotel. In more recent times, literary history was made
when Edith Wharton stayed at the Charing Cross Hotel in 1909.

It is a fine railway hotel catering for tourists and
businessmen who no doubt appreciate its superbly convenient situation in the Strand near Trafalgar Square. From
the hotel can be seen the National Gallery and St Martin in the
Fields. The Houses of Parliament and Westminster Abbey,
Covent Garden and Whitehall—all are nearby. Theatres and
restaurants are within walking distance of the hotel.

Shortly after the hotel was built in 1864, an annexe of ninety

Edith Wharton (1862–1937) and The Charing Cross Hotel, London, where she stayed with her lover, William Morton Fullerton bedrooms was added and connected to the main building by a footbridge across Villiers Street. A further structural change was necessitated when, during World War II, enemy bombardment on the night of 16 April 1941 damaged the hotel. Restored in 1951, the original mansard roof was replaced by a new and modern top storey.

The hotel is large, efficient and moderately-priced. Its 206 rooms are comfortably furnished and each has a television and tea-making facilities, while the hotel also has such amenities as a sauna and gentlemen's hairdressing. It has two bars and a residents' lounge as well as another literary connection—its Betjeman Restaurant, named for the Poet Laureate. Sir John Betjeman has indicated his fondness for the Charing Cross Hotel and has dined frequently at what he has called a 'most finely appointed hotel dining room'. He has also singled out the grand staircase with its inviting 'broad carpeted stairs' that make a pleasant climb to the first floor where the principal rooms are located—the Italian Renaissance style restaurant with original corner columns, the lounge in similar style and banqueting rooms.

It is most appropriate to think of the Charing Cross Hotel in terms of its literary guest of distinction—the remarkable Edith Wharton.

Born in aristocratic old New York City on 24 January 1862, Edith Newbold Jones became Edith Wharton when, at the spinsterish age of twenty-three, she married Edward (Teddy) Wharton, twelve years her senior. Within a few years, the marriage began to show signs of disintegration and Edith turned to writing, perhaps as an outlet.

Teddy Wharton was an ineffectual man with no vocation and no real interests. Edith was becoming a self-assured and forceful personality and was beginning to establish a reputation as a writer. Clearly, she had outgrown her non-intellectual husband, who was also showing symptoms of mental illness. His increasingly severe manic-depressive condition finally led to a divorce in 1913, after nearly thirty years of marriage.

Edith Wharton's first book was published in 1897 when she collaborated with her architect-friend, Ogden Codman, on a volume called *The Decoration of Houses*. Walter Berry, a distant cousin, helped her with the style and organisation and remained her lifelong friend and mentor. Her understanding of the need for proportion and balance in architecture and her impeccable good taste came to the fore when she designed and built her home in Lenox, Massachusetts, in 1900. When Henry James came to stay at The Mount, as the country home of the Whartons was called, he described it in a letter as 'a delicate French chateau mirrored in a Massachusetts pond'.

Best known as a writer of novels and short stories, Edith had published the first of her eighty-six short stories in 1891. Berry encouraged and advised her in the fiction she wrote, and they remained close friends always.

Edith's circle of friends, invariably men, included Henry James. When they first met at a dinner party in Paris, the young Edith Wharton was overawed by the famous author and too timid to converse with him. Over a dozen years later, when he was living at Lamb House in Rye, their friendship developed into a warm and extremely close relationship that lasted until his death. She visited him often at Lamb House on her frequent trips to England. She was also often entertained at the home of Howard Sturgis, Queen's Acre, in Windsor.

For someone who had no need to work, Edith Wharton made the difficult choice of becoming a writer. She applied discipline to her craft and wrote regularly each morning. *The Valley of Decision*, her first novel, appeared in 1902 when she was forty. She was still at work on a novel in 1937, at the time of her death on 11 August, and *The Buccaneers* was published posthumously.

In between came such novels as *The House of Mirth* (1905), *Ethan Frome* (1911), *The Reef* (1912), *The Custom of the Country* (1913) and *The Age of Innocence* (1920), for which she won the Pulitzer Prize.

In Europe, Edith found the sympathetic and literary people

she needed. She had looked for a house in England and considered settling in the country Henry James had chosen for his home, but she felt dissatisfied and took up residence in France, reserving England as a holiday place. Rye and Windsor were her two main retreats on her frequent visits to England for a good time.

In June 1909, Edith Wharton took a holiday in London with William Morton Fullerton, and they stayed at the Charing Cross Hotel. The story of Fullerton is the story of the single true love of her life.

She originally met Fullerton, an American journalist who was based in Paris as a correspondent for the London *Times*, at her home in Lenox in 1907. She had returned to The Mount from an exciting tour abroad which had included a round of parties, dinners and gay Paris life, as well as a motoring expedition through France in which she was joined by Henry James. Fullerton was now on a visit to America, and his friend Henry James arranged the meeting at Lenox. Fullerton was an extremely attractive, sensual man with a long and involved history of becoming entangled with the women he captivated.

He captivated Edith. She was forty-five and he, forty-two. Magical feelings were mutually kindled and, after he left, Edith began to keep a private journal addressed to him, but not intended for his eyes. In the diary, she expressed the longing to be to Fullerton 'like a touch of wings brushing by you in the darkness, or like the scent of an invisible garden that one passes by on an unknown road.' She also moved forward the date of her projected return to France and left in December.

Naturally, their friendship resumed in Paris. In the year 1908, she continued to write and to lead a remarkably busy social life. But she found time to be alone with him—some hours in the country, a quiet lunch, a gallery exhibition. She was simply, and discreetly, in love. Henry James came over, his last time in France, and the three enjoyed a good time together.

[28]

Her love for Fullerton deepened. By the spring of 1908, her conflicts over morality and adultery and her puritanical concern for order in society seemed resolved. Their friendship was fused into a passionate, physical union.

Her writing went well. A fourth volume of short stories was published in September 1908, *The Hermit and the Wild Woman,* followed in October by *A Motor-Flight Through France.* Her first collection of poems, *Artemis to Actaeon,* appeared in April 1909, and at least ten of the poems in that volume were based on her relationship with Fullerton. Edith Wharton often used incidents, people and places she knew in her writing.

On 3 June 1909, she and Fullerton crossed the Channel to Folkestone, where they spent the night. In London the next day, they took Suite 92, two bedrooms and a sitting room, at the Charing Cross Hotel. Henry James joined them there for dinner, and they spent a gay evening with dim red lights, champagne and good conversation. After James left, the two had a passionate night. Fullerton was scheduled to leave for America in the morning to visit his parents.

In the morning, alone after Fullerton had gone, Edith sat propped up in bed writing, as was her wont. But this time she did not write fiction. She wrote a fifty-two-line poem. *Terminus* is the name of the erotic poem which she composed that morning about the night before. The title cleverly suggests a station hotel as well as a temporary end to their relationship. It begins with amazing candour:

Wonderful was the long secret night you gave me, my Lover,
Palm to palm, breast to breast in the gloom. The faint red lamp
Flushing with magical shadows the common-place room of
    the inn,
With its dull impersonal furniture, kindled a mystic flame
In the heart of the swinging mirror . . .

That afternoon, she and James drove to Queen's Acre where she stayed for ten days before going back to London and another social whirl. When Fullerton returned from America, they spent another night in London, then went for a motor tour with Henry James in her chauffeur-driven car before the pair returned to Paris. James was sixty-six and exhausted.

The *Terminus* incident is fictionalised at the Terminus Hotel in Paris in *The Reef* (1912). In that novel, Sophy Viner and George Darrow consummate their passion in a Paris station hotel near the Gare du Nord, during a spring rain (it had rained in London), in a room that is reminiscent of the one at the Charing Cross Hotel: '. . . the grimy carpet and wall-paper, the black marble mantel-piece, the clock with a gilt allegory under a dusty bell, the high-bolstered brown-counterpaned bed, the framed card of printed rules under the electric light switch, and the door of communication with the next room.'

Paradoxically, the writer who worked assiduously to preserve her privacy, who guarded it even in her auto-biography, left bits of her private life scattered throughout the novel. But who could know the significance of the fictional account? Or the truth of the poem?

If the tone of the novel is different, and somewhat seedier, that is because the Edith Wharton of 1912 looked back with distaste. The affair that began in the autumn of 1907 ended in the summer of 1910. His three-year span of attention to a love relationship was almost over. Her impossible situation caus-ed her to become disenchanted. Perhaps with Teddy's own adulterous adventures now revealed, she felt obliged to measure them both by the same moral standards. In any event, the affair petered out. He ceased to be the man of her dreams but remained the attractive man she had loved and who had loved her in return.

After The Mount was sold in 1911, and after her divorce, France became the permanent home of Edith Wharton. From Paris, she moved to the Pavillon Colombe, just twelve miles north of the city, and later she had a winter home at Hyères on the French Riviera. During World War I, she ran missions for refugees, for which she was awarded the Legion of Honour.

She returned to the United States only once, in 1923, when she was awarded an honorary doctorate from Yale University—the first woman to be so honoured. This was a singularly appropriate tribute to the writer who frequently dealt with the intricacies of the lives of women who are victims in a world made for men. Her illumination of those issues and her intense psychological probing continue to be appropriate.

E. M. FORSTER

at

THE KINGSLEY HOTEL
BLOOMSBURY WAY
LONDON WC1

And even more curious was the drawing-
room, which attempted to rival the solid
comfort of a Bloomsbury boarding-house.
Was this really Italy?

A Room with a View

The Kingsley Hotel in Bloomsbury is an unpretentious, unimposing, moderately-priced hotel located very near the British Museum. The red-brick building with turrets at each end was built at the turn of the century. The year of its inception, 1900, is inscribed on the façade high above the front door. A reception hall with pillars and two crystal chandeliers leads to a large and comfortable lounge for residents on the left. With its fireplace and stuffed chairs and sofas, the room is the epitome of 'solid comfort'.

Also on the ground floor is the dining room known as 'The Carver'. A lift makes the ascent to six upper floors with a total of 169 bedrooms, most with private bathrooms. But before the addition of a wing in 1926, the front section of the original hotel consisted of only a hundred rooms.

Opposite the lounge is the plush Bloomsbury Bar and the Thackeray Room, used for conferences and named for the author of *Vanity Fair*. The hotel itself was named for another writer, Charles Kingsley, remembered for such works as *Westward Ho!* and *The Water-Babies*. But apparent literary interest stops short of honouring the author who actually lived in this pleasant hotel.

E. M. Forster
(1879–1970) (in Indian
costume) and the
Kingsley Hotel,
London, where he
lodged with his mother

Long before E. M. Forster wrote his well-known novels, long before he became part of the Bloomsbury group of artists and intellectuals, he came to the Kingsley Hotel. In fact he and his mother took up residence at the hotel while seeking a place to live.

The story begins however with the birth of Edward Morgan Forster on 1 January 1879 and the death of his father twenty-two months later. He was brought up in a world of women and adored the over-protective mother who dominated him throughout her life. Alice Clara Forster moved with four-year-old Morgan to a house near Stevenage in Hertfordshire called 'Rooksnest', the prototype for the house which gave his fourth novel its title, *Howards End*. Already he was coming into contact with places and incidents which were to be adapted as elements in his novels.

They were forced to leave that beloved house when he was fourteen, and the boy entered the detested Tonbridge School. His hatred for it is expressed when it is described as Sawston School in *The Longest Journey*.

At seventeen he entered King's College, Cambridge, where he found happiness and freedom. His college rooms became the setting for the discussion on the nature of reality in *The Longest Journey*.

After leaving Cambridge, with no career in mind, he decided to embark on the almost obligatory grand tour of Europe. Fortunately, a private income allowed him to seek personal fulfilment without the immediate need to take on a permanent profession. With his mother, he left England in October 1901. Notes he made in Italy of people, places, and events became the bases for several early novels. San Gimignano, for instance, was the Monteriano of *Where Angels Fear to Tread*.

On their return to England a year later, mother and son settled into the newly-built Kingsley Hotel while trying to form definite plans. The Kingsley Hotel had the advantage of proximity to the Working Men's College in Great Ormond Street where Forster taught a weekly class in Latin.

The following spring, with no prospect yet of regular employment, son and mother went on another tour of the Continent. But this time, he went on a Greek cruise while she stayed in Florence for a holiday of her own. He joined her after the tour of Greece was over. In Florence, they attended a performance of Donizetti's opera, *Lucia di Lammermoor*, with the soprano Tetrazzini singing the leading role. The event later made its way into *Where Angels Fear to Tread* as an effective little scene.

The two travellers returned to England in August 1903 and again stayed at the Kingsley while searching for a place to live. In the spring of 1904, they took a flat in South Kensington and exchanged it after some months for a house in Weybridge—their home for the next twenty years. They moved in 1924 to Abinger Hammer in Surrey, their home until Alice Forster's death.

It might be said that Forster bloomed in Bloomsbury, for it was during his stay at the Kingsley Hotel that he began to contribute essays and stories to the *Independent Review* and wrote parts of his early Italian novels. When he checked into the hotel, his luggage contained the inspiration provided by his visits to Europe. He began the writing of *A Room with a View*, but *Where Angels Fear to Tread* was published first, in 1905. This successful novel was followed by *The Longest Journey* (1907), *A Room with a View* (1908), *Howards End* (1910) and, after a long hiatus, *A Passage to India* (1924).

His links with Bloomsbury are further emphasised by his affiliation with the Bloomsbury circle of friends with Cambridge or family ties. He reviewed Virginia Woolf's first novel of 1915, *The Voyage Out*, with unbounded admiration. He later praised *To the Lighthouse* and thought it her best novel. Although they remained good friends until her death, Virginia Woolf frequently criticised his works in print. In one article, she discussed the failure of Forster's work to reconcile realism wth vision because of a too-literal rendition of too much observation. In a review of his series of lectures published as *Aspects of the Novel*, she differed with him on the concept of 'Life'.

Aspects of the Novel emanated from the distinguished series of Clark Lectures which Trinity College, Cambridge invited Forster to deliver in 1927 and thus re-established his Cambridge connection. The success of the eight lectures led to their publication and to his being offered a three-year fellowship at King's College.

Forster had a long life and a varied career which included reviewing and editing as well as the writing of short stories, important books of criticism and essays, two biographies and travel books. During World War I, he served with the International Red Cross in Alexandria as a 'searcher', which involved the gathering of information about 'missing' soldiers. The literary yield of the years spent in Egypt were *Alexandria: A History and a Guide* and *Pharos and Pharillon*, a collection of essays.

His travels took him to India in 1912 and again in 1921 as private secretary to the Maharaja of Dewas. *The Hill of Devi*, about his experiences in Dewas, proclaimed his two visits to be 'the great opportunity of my life'. It was after his second trip to India that the novel generally accepted as his masterpiece appeared in 1924—*A Passage to India*. (There was to be a third visit to India in October 1945 for a conference of writers.)

Forster's myriad activities included serving as president of the National Council for Civil Liberties and broadcasting for the BBC. After the death of his mother in 1945, King's College elected him to an Honorary Fellowship and gave him rooms at the college, where he lived for the last twenty-five years of his life.

He collaborated with Ralph Vaughan Williams on a pageant and wrote the libretto for Benjamin Britten's opera, *Billy Budd*. And he did continue to create fiction during the apparent periods of silence. He remained an active writer until nearly the end, which came on 6 June 1970. And after the end, came the posthumous works: *Maurice*, the novel about homosexual love, was begun in 1913 and published in 1971. A collection of short stories with the chilling choice of title for a posthumous volume, *The Life to Come,* appeared in 1972.

Despite Forster's immense versatility, his reputation rests primarily on his novels. In the early years of his development as a novelist, the fame that this gentle person never sought, sought him—and found him writing at the Kingsley Hotel in Bloomsbury.

JANE AUSTEN

at

THE ROYAL VICTORIA AND BULL HOTEL
I HIGH STREET
DARTFORD
KENT

> They were three days on their journey . . .
> They reached town by three o'clock the third
> day, glad to be released, after such a journey,
> from the confinement of a carriage, and ready
> · to enjoy all the luxury of a good fire.

Sense and Sensibility

In the Middle Ages, when Dartford was Darentford, huge numbers of pilgrims forded the River Darent at this convenient stopping place on their first night out from London. Through the apple and cherry orchards of Kent they continued, on the so-called Pilgrim's Way, to their destination—Canterbury Cathedral. Thomas à Becket was murdered in the cathedral in 1170, and his martyrdom and canonisation gave rise to the most popular pilgrimage in Britain. Countless numbers rode out to the shrine, 'the hooly blisful martir for to seke' (as Chaucer says in *The Canterbury Tales*).

Few pilgrims visit Dartford today. A place that is normally and understandably avoided by tourists, modern Dartford is an industrial town with a landscape that includes factories and smoking chimneys and with a population that accounts for urban sprawl and commuters. But at least one old-world feature exists to make the short journey from London worthwhile—the Royal Victoria and Bull.

Formerly known as The Bull, the name of this important old coaching inn was changed after the accession of Queen

Once called the Bull, now The Royal Victoria and Bull, Dartford, this old coaching inn is where Jane Austen stayed after visiting her brother in Kent

The Dover–London Stage Coach

Victoria, who visited it on several occasions. Once a number of inns stood in the main street, and this majestic inn is not to be confused with the smaller one (no longer in existence) nearly opposite called the Bull and George. The use of the word 'Bull' is ancient; one theory is that its derivation is ecclesiastical and originates from the bulla or seal given by a priory to a place which housed its visitors.

That Jane Austen, like those ancient Canterbury pilgrims, spent the first night out at Dartford after a visit to her brother's family in Kent, that she spent it in a unique and pleasant hotel, would seem to be reason enough to revive the tourist industry of Dartford.

Jane Austen's life appears to be geographically restricted. She was born on 16 December 1775 in the village of Steventon in Hampshire where she spent the first twenty-six years of life. Then with her father's retirement, the family moved to Bath where she lived for the next five years. In 1806, the year after her father's death, her widowed mother moved to Southampton with her two daughters before finally settling in Chawton in Hampshire in 1809. There Jane remained for the last eight years of her life, except for the final days. She was taken to Winchester to be given medical care when her health failed. Death came on 18 July 1817, and she is buried in Winchester Cathedral, where a memorial inscription pays tribute:

> The benevolence of her heart, the sweetness of her temper, and the extraordinary endowments of her mind obtained the regard of all who knew her and the warmest love of her intimate connections.

Significantly, it refers to Jane Austen the beloved human being, not to Jane Austen the beloved author whose books have brought joy to so many.

Although she never travelled abroad, Jane Austen, like the characters in her novels, did a great deal of travelling to English places, particularly to holiday resorts in the south such as Sidmouth, Lyme Regis and Charmouth. Concerned with accuracy, Jane was not tempted to write about areas outside the realm of her experience. Her novels dealt only with the places she knew and with the people she knew to inhabit them. So naturalistic is her writing, and so strongly is the reality felt by readers, that when Tennyson was being shown the site where the Duke of Monmouth landed in Lyme Regis, he impatiently responded to his friend: 'Don't talk to me of Monmouth. Show me the exact spot where Louisa Musgrave fell!'

Jane Austen visited London frequently to see a favourite brother, Henry, and both she and her elder sister Cassandra made journeys to Kent to visit their brother Edward.

Edward had been adopted (like Frank Churchill in *Emma*) by a distant cousin, Thomas Knight. Mr and Mrs Knight had no children of their own and no heir to their fortune. After Thomas Knight died in 1794, Edward took over the fine eighteenth-century Palladian mansion known as Godmersham Park and later the name of Knight as well. The house lies in the beautiful valley of the Stour only eight miles from Canterbury. Between 1794 and 1813, Jane was often at Godmersham enjoying the country-house society and the life of leisure of the more affluent branch of the Austen family. Both sisters enjoyed the spacious mansion filled with loving children and the superb setting with garden and deer park.

Conditions of travel were arduous, and a good inn to break the journey was essential. Jane passed through Dartford many times on her way to or from Godmersham. She stayed in Dartford on a number of occasions in the nineteen-year period when she was making journeys into East Kent, sometimes arranging to take advantage of the good inn in Dartford. In a letter of 17 January 1809 she expresses the intention to sleep at Dartford: 'There certainly does seem no convenient resting place on the other road.'

It seems likely, therefore, that she would choose the best inn in Dartford—the old Bull (which later became the Royal Victoria and Bull). But there is confusion over the profusion of Dartford inns. An oft-quoted letter of 24 October 1798, written when she and her mother were returning to Steventon (having left Cassandra behind to help care for the children of Edward and Elizabeth), is headed from the Bull and George —the inn across the road. Even then conversation about the weather took precedence: 'We had one heavy shower on leaving Sittingbourne, but afterwards the clouds cleared away and we had a very bright *chrystal* afternoon.'

She went on to describe an unsettling incident in which her luggage was sent off in error: 'After we had been here a quarter of an hour it was discovered that my writing and dressing boxes had been by accident put into a chaise which was just packing off as we came in, and were driven away towards Gravesend on their way to the West Indies.' A man on horseback was speedily sent out to retrieve the boxes.

David Waldron Smithers, an authority on Jane Austen in Kent, offers the plausible explanation that the favoured inn, the Bull, had no rooms available on that particular occasion, and so they had to put up over the road. Other letters refer to the Bull, as in this extract from a letter of June 1808: 'At Dartford, which we reached within the two hours and three-quarters, we went to the Bull, the same inn at which we breakfasted in that said journey, and on the present occasion had about the same bad butter. At half-past ten we were again off . . . and by six o'clock were at Godmersham.'

Nowadays the butter is better at the old Bull, which remains the best hotel in Dartford. This old coaching inn retains its medieval gallery which overlooks the courtyard, in which stands an authentic nineteenth-century coach. The courtyard, now covered over by a glass roof, is a superb example of one of the few surviving galleried inn courtyards in the land. Fourteen rooms are located around the gallery, and an additional twenty bedrooms were added in a 1973 extension. It is still a fine hotel with large and comfortable bedrooms and central location in the town.

The visitor might well pause for reflection in the courtyard, with its long history which dates back to about 1450. The reason for the author's presence at this establishment—her visits to Kent—had a definite influence on her writing. The experiences of these journeys provided her with knowledge of people, of society, of the interactions of family groups, as well as of activities of great houses. The insights are there to be treasured in her novels.

Sense and Sensibility, her first book, was written in 1798 and revised and published in 1811. She was by then journeying into Kent, and the book contains many references to travel. *Pride and Prejudice* and *Northanger Abbey* belong also to the first period of great creativity. She paid her last visit to Kent in 1813, the year in which she completed *Mansfield Park*. *Emma* was completed in 1815 and *Persuasion*, in 1816.

Although her output was small, although so little is known of her, the feeling of closeness to Jane Austen and her six novels is intensified in the presence of such associations in the Kentish setting from which her genius flowed. Even today, a pilgrimage to Kent with a stop at the Royal Victoria and Bull in Dartford can open vistas into her world.

SIR ARTHUR CONAN DOYLE

at

UNDERSHAW HOTEL
HINDHEAD
SURREY

. . . he had settled in modest comfort into the
old house of Cosford upon the eastern slope of
the Hindhead hill.

Sir Nigel

To follow in the footsteps of Sherlock Holmes, aficionados often seek out the fictional premises at 221B Baker Street. Letters still pour into that non-existent Baker Street address. But anyone wishing to follow in the footsteps of the creator of the world's most acclaimed detective can go to the actual abode of Arthur Conan Doyle at Hindhead in Surrey.

'Home of the late Sir Arthur Conan Doyle' are the words on the sign outside the Undershaw Hotel. Accompanying those words is a silhouette of the famous detective, complete with pipe, magnifying glass and deerstalker cap. The facts relating to how Undershaw came to be Conan Doyle's home are elementary.

Born in Edinburgh in 1859, Arthur Conan Doyle went to Edinburgh University where he received medical training as well as basic training for the stories he was later to write. He was influenced by a certain Dr Joseph Bell, a fascinating lecturer who used an intriguing method of deductive reasoning to diagnose cases. Eventually, Conan Doyle set up a medical practice in Southsea on the Hampshire coast. There, in 1885, the struggling young doctor married Louise Hawkins, whose dying brother he had been treating.

Undershaw Hotel, Hindhead, 'a considerable mansion', built to Sir Arthur Conan Doyle's (1859–1930) own specifications and his home for many years

Even in those early days, he tried his hand at writing. Literary success came with his brilliant idea of using a detective who would rely on logic and science to reconstruct a crime, a detective whose methods were reminiscent of those of Dr Bell. As Sherrinford Holmes evolved to become Sherlock Holmes, as his friend Dr James Watson became Dr John H. Watson, and as *A Tangled Skein* became *A Study in Scarlet*, Arthur Conan Doyle became the creator of one of the most celebrated characters in English literature.

Although not financially successful at first, a literary career was launched. By 1891, Conan Doyle decided to give up his medical practice and turn himself entirely to writing.

Louise was diagnosed, in 1893, as having tuberculosis and given only a few months to live. She remained in a delicate state of health for the next thirteen years. To prolong her life, the couple went to live in Switzerland. Meanwhile, he continued to write and to travel and even managed to go on an American speaking tour.

The return to England, which they both longed for, was made possible by the writer Grant Allen, himself a victim of tuberculosis. Allen believed in the therapeutic qualities of Surrey as a safe place for sufferers of the disease. Doyle investigated. He wrote that the place would be suitable for her recuperation 'because its height, its dryness, its sandy soil, its fir-trees, and its shelter from all bitter winds present the conditions which all agree to be best.'

He decided to have a house built at Hindhead and hired a Southsea architect and old friend to build a 'considerable mansion' to his own specifications. The ambitious plan indicated a considerable change in his financial position compared with the early years in Southsea, when he polished up the brass plate on his own front door. The desire to return to England was fulfilled. In October 1897, he and Louise were able to move into Undershaw, as the house was named in a reference to its position below or under a *shaw*, the Old English word for a small wood or thicket.

Undershaw was a large and comfortable house, and Conan

Doyle continued to work, write and give readings. In addition to his literary labours, he took advantage of available country sports and enjoyed the open air and the fields. He also laid out a tennis court in the grounds.

Here, in his study, he resurrected Sherlock Holmes. Earlier, he had arranged for the demise of his hero in *The Final Problem* when, together with the evil Professor Moriarty, Holmes is killed as he disappears over the edge into the Reichenbach Falls in Switzerland. Having achieved literary fame and financial success, Conan Doyle had tired of the immortal figure who had taken over his life. He wanted to get on with other works. 'I am weary of his name,' he wrote in a letter to his mother, the 'Ma'am' as the formidable lady was addressed.

But the public complained. At Undershaw Conan Doyle did much of the writing of *The Hound of the Baskervilles* with Sherlock Holmes back as the detective-hero. Chronologically, however, that story is set before the death of Sherlock Holmes. Perhaps one reason for the knighthood of Sir Arthur in 1902 was gratitude for the return of the popular detective. The public lamented and the author relented. In 1903, in *The Adventure of the Empty House*, Holmes returned alive and well and living at 221B Baker Street with the explanation, not that he had survived the fall into the chasm, but that he never fell at all. He had climbed to safety on the other side of the cliff, unbeknown to Watson.

Conan Doyle's historical novel *Sir Nigel*, also written at Undershaw, shows an easy familiarity with the Surrey scene as young Nigel journeys along the Pilgrims' Way to Dover: 'To their left was a hilly country, a land of rolling heaths and woods, broken here and there into open spaces round the occasional farmhouse of a franklin. Hackhurst Down, Dunley Hill, and Ranmore Common swelled and sank, each merging into the other. But on the right, after passing the village of Shere and the old church of Gomshall, the whole south country lay like a map at their feet.'

After Louise died in 1906, he married Jean Leckie whom he

had met much earlier, in 1897, and whom he deeply loved. But he had remained true to his chivalrous standards and loyal to his invalid wife. Just a year after the death of Louise, he married Jean and moved to a new home at Crowborough in Sussex, where he remained until his death on 11 July 1930, at the age of seventy-one. Undershaw was sold.

The Undershaw Hotel is located forty-two miles south of London within easy reach of two busy roads (the A3 from London and the A287 from Haslemere, two miles to the east). But trees and shrubbery surround it so effectively that neither sight nor sound of traffic is disturbing. The south side of the hotel overlooks the Nutcombe Valley to the hills of the South Downs, and the beautiful view is enhanced in the springtime when framed by rhododendrons, ablaze in colour. The wrought iron gate through which the red-brick hotel may be approached incorporates the name 'Undershaw' and the initials 'ACD'.

Inside is further evidence of the Arthur Conan Doyle connection. In the hall is the great stained-glass window with heraldic shields of the Doyle family. Somehow, he had forgotten to include the arms of his mother's ancestors. To placate the angry Ma'am, that coat of arms was quickly installed in the window over the main staircase.

Brass finger plates on the doors incorporate his monogram. Door handles need only be gently pushed, not twisted or turned, his own specification to make door opening easy for Louise, whose hands were crippled by arthritis. Shallow stairs also made movement easier for her arthritic limbs. Spacious and well-lit rooms include the study where he wrote much of his material.

It is all there. To remember Sir Arthur Conan Doyle, forget Baker Street. Go to the place where the famous Baskerville hound first bayed—go to Undershaw.

JOHN KEATS

at

THE BURFORD BRIDGE HOTEL
DORKING
SURREY

O thou wouldst joy to live in such a place.

Endymion

Would John Keats have finished his long *Endymion* if he had not secluded himself in a hotel at the foot of Box Hill? Probably. But although the answer may remain forever uncertain, what is certain is the fact that he went there with the explicit purpose of completing *Endymion* and proving himself as a poet.

He started the long classical legend of Endymion and the Moon-goddess around October 1816, having chosen this haunting story to be a test of his poetic ability. He dated the poem 16 December and left it unfinished. But this successful beginning, together with the success of his earlier first volume of poems, led to a turning point. He made the final and irrevocable decision to end his career in medicine and to devote himself to poetry.

He had always had an intense interest in language and poetry. When John Keats was eight, his father died as the result of a fall from his horse, and when he was not quite fifteen, his mother died of tuberculosis. John, born on 31 October 1795, the eldest of the four Keats children, was withdrawn from school by his guardian and apprenticed to a surgeon and apothecary. The orphan had to be able to earn a living.

His apprenticeship over, he entered Guy's Hospital for a six-month term which would qualify him to practise. He completed the course, passed the examination in July 1816, and needed only to wait for his twenty-first birthday before he could legally set up his own practice. In the interim, he could prepare for his profession. But instead of gaining further experience at Guy's, he went to the fashionable seaside resort of Margate, where he could be free to write.

Weeks passed and so did his birthday, but he took no action toward establishing a professional opening. Success with such poems as *On First Looking into Chapman's Homer, I Stood Tiptoe* and *Sleep and Poetry* helped to seal his fate. Before long, he was inextricably involved with a four-thousand-line poem, *Endymion*.

Progress on the projected four books of *Endymion* went slowly, and he digressed from time to time to other poems. In the spring of 1817, he went to the Isle of Wight and worked on Book Two, and in the autumn, feeling that a change of scene would be beneficial to the creative process, he accepted an invitation to go to Oxford to write Book Three. He still had another book to go, and his rate of writing slowed down considerably. He had hoped to have it finished by autumn, but winter was now fast approaching. At the start of the poem, he expressed the hope,

> O may no wintry season, bare and hoary
> See it half finished; but let Autumn bold,
> With universal tinge of sober gold,
> Be all about me when I make an end.

Only one solution was possible. He needed to get away again, as he wrote in a letter to his friend Benjamin Bailey, 'to change the Scene—change the Air and give me a spur to wind up my Poem, of which there are wanting 500 Lines.'

So, about a year after he first started *Endymion*, he found a quiet retreat a mere twenty miles from London to which he escaped to complete the long poem. The Fox and Hounds, as the inn was then called, was situated in Surrey about one mile north of Dorking, between that village and Leatherhead. He

John Keats
(1795–1821) and The
Burford Bridge
Hotel, under Boxhill
where he completed
his poem 'Endymion'

arrived at the old coaching inn on 22 November 1817. From then, events proceeded with fairy-tale success toward a happy conclusion.

The low white building now stands in a garden of two acres, amidst beautiful scenery. About fifty feet behind it is the hill which takes its name from the box trees which grow on it. Box Hill rises steeply to a height of almost five hundred feet. In fact, only box and yew trees can keep hold in the steep western slopes near Burford Bridge. Before the hotel, spreads the Mickleham Valley with its little River Mole, a weed-choked river spanned by the three arches of the stone Burford Bridge and described by the poet Alexander Pope as 'the sullen Mole, that hides his diving flood'. It tends to disappear in dry seasons and flow underground.

Keats stayed in a small back room overlooking the stable yard. The bedroom window gives a view of lawn with fine old trees, a beech and a cedar. How he must have admired the scene which, with a large garden at the back, with a hermit's grotto or summerhouse, made him feel at once comfortably at home and free from worry. He must have been excited also by the fact that his room was next to one that had been occupied by his boyhood hero, Admiral Nelson. Nelson stayed here when he took his last farewell of Lady Hamilton before the Battle of Trafalgar.

From a path behind the inn, Keats climbed Box Hill. He could slip through the garden gate near the hermitage to walk up the hill through the box and yew trees to look down into the peaceful valley. Exhilarated by the natural scenery, he climbed up the hill the first night and returned with a flow of inspired lines. Extremely happy in his quiet new environment, he wrote in a letter: 'I like this place very much. There is Hill & Dale and a little River—I went up Box Hill this Evening after the Moon—you 'a seen the Moon—came down —and wrote some lines.'

And these are the lines he wrote:

The moon put forth a little diamond peak,
No bigger than an unobserved star,
Or tiny point of fairy scimitar;
Bright signal that she only stooped to tie
Her silver sandals, ere deliciously
She bowed into the heavens her timid head.

Like his hero Endymion, faced with failure and immersed in troubles, he had entered the cave of quietude and emerged renewed.

Lines from *Endymion* describe the autumnal beauty of Box Hill:

Where shall our dwelling be? Under the brow
Of some steep mossy hill, where ivy dun
Would hide us up, although spring leaves were none;
And where dark yew trees, as we rustle through,
Will drop their scarlet berry cups of dew?
O thou wouldst joy to live in such a place.

Keats joyed to live in this place. He continued to write. Confining himself to his small room for most of the day, he wrote an average of eighty to eighty-five lines a day. *Endymion*, with its familiar first line, 'A thing of beauty is a joy for ever,' was soon finished. The place and date—Burford Bridge, 28 November 1817—were appended to the draft of Book Four. In a state of elation following completion of this large work which he had chosen to prove his ability, he stayed on for another week. Before he left Burford Bridge, he produced a very moving lyric, 'In a drear-nighted December'. He emerged as a true poet. He was twenty-two.

The sensuous delights, the music, so melodious and rhythmically satisfying, the richness of imagery—these qualities make Keats one of the greatest of English poets. *Hyperion, The Eve of St Agnes*, the great odes—*Ode to Psyche, Ode to a Nightingale, Ode on a Grecian Urn, To Autumn*—so full of emotional intensity, sensation and artistry, have found a permanent place in literature and in the hearts of an appreciative public.

But his was to be a tragically short life. As his literary power ascended, his health and happiness descended. One of his brothers emigrated to the United States. Another died young of tuberculosis. Keats, too, contracted the fatal disease. The illness caused a self-imposed separation from his beloved Fanny Brawne and made marriage impossible. It sent him to Italy in search of a more beneficial climate, but he died in Rome on 23 February 1821. He was twenty-five.

The Box Hill experience must be remembered as a peak period of happiness in his life. Now modernised and given a straightforward name, the Burford Bridge Hotel, a rambling building with fifty-two bedrooms, offers informal public rooms and high standards of comfort throughout. It still nestles near the River Mole under the steep side of Box Hill, now preserved by the National Trust and it is still a popular place for walks and picnics—as it was for Jane Austen, who selected Box Hill as the setting for an excursion in *Emma*, which ended so disastrously when the heroine was unkind to Miss Bates.

A visitor to this place may very well write a postcard using Keats's own words, 'I like this place very much.'

EDWARD LEAR

at

OATLANDS PARK HOTEL
WEYBRIDGE
SURREY

How pleasant to know Mr Lear!
Who has written such volumes of stuff!
Some think him ill-tempered and queer,
But a few think him pleasant enough.

Self Portrait in *Nonsense Songs and Stories* (1895)

The pleasant enough master of the nonsense rhyme was born on 12 May 1812, in the district of London known as Holloway. He was an unattractive child with poor vision and poor health, who suffered also from epilepsy. The youngest of a large family of twenty-one children, he was rejected by his over-burdened mother and placed in the care of his sister Ann when he was four and she was twenty-five. Ann looked after him with great concern and affection for the rest of her life, making an excellent surrogate mother until her death in 1861 at the age of seventy.

Edward Lear began to earn a living from his drawings when he was fifteen, but it was as an ornithological artist that he achieved a reputation for accuracy and for beauty of design and execution. His first regular employment came when the Zoological Society hired him to make drawings of the parrots at the Regent's Park Zoo. It was also due to his profession as an artist that he became, inadvertently, a popular and professional nonsense writer.

In 1832, the Earl of Derby, impressed with Lear's work at the Zoo, invited him to the ancient and great family estate of Knowsley Hall near Liverpool to make illustrations of his

[55]

unique collection of animals and birds. During the years spent at Knowsley, Lear earned the lifelong patronage and friendship of the noble family, who gave its name to the well-known horse race. More importantly, Lear's career as writer dates from that same period: he amused the children of the house with his silly rhymes, and the nonsense he made up for the Knowsley children was eventually published. The results of four years of work were printed in a private edition in 1846, *Gleanings from the Menagerie and Aviary at Knowsley Hall*; but that same year also saw the publication of Lear's *A Book of Nonsense,* a book which brought him the lasting fame that eluded him as an artist.

A second edition of his *Book of Nonsense* appeared ten years later, and Lear offered to sell the copyright for one hundred pounds. But his publishers were unwilling to take the risk. When a third edition of two thousand copies followed in 1861 and sold out immediately, the publishers changed their minds, but Lear shrewdly, he thought, raised the price. Not appreciating its potential and value, he sold the copyright for a mere £125, the total profit realised for a book that went into nearly thirty editions in his own lifetime.

The theme of the loss of happiness is prevalent in the first *Book of Nonsense* and in others which followed. His Owl and Pussy-Cat seek contentment in a faraway land where they dine on mince and slices of quince with a runcible spoon and dance by the light of the moon. Other characters escape to the great Gromboolian plain or to the hills of the Chankly Bore, full of a haunting mystery.

Like his characters, Lear sought escape. His poor state of health plagued him throughout life, although he lived to be seventy-six. In particular, he suffered from chronic asthma and bronchitis, exacerbated by the English climate. Escape to warmer weather, at least in the winter time, could only be advantageous. Moreover, he reasoned, southern climes could provide him with exotic scenes to paint. Unaware that nonsense was his metier, he made the conscious decision to earn his livelihood as a landscape painter. Painting landscapes

Edward Lear (1812–1888)

Oatlands Park Hotel, Weybridge
(below)
Lear feeding 'unfortunate birds at
Oatlands Park Hotel' (bottom)

would also conserve his poor vision which was strained by the minute details required in drawing birds and animals.

He left for Italy in July 1837 and was henceforth to live a peripatetic life. He returned frequently to England at intervals, but largely spent his life abroad where he continued to draw or paint and to write. His journeys became professional searches for the picturesque which would yield landscapes that he could sell. He was willing to endure discomforts to obtain a sketch he wanted. Italy, Corfu, Albania, Greece, Corsica, Malta, Egypt, Crete, Palestine—these became his terrain for the rich supply of subject matter.

In addition to excursions into picturesque scenes and countries, he took occasional excursions into writing. He published over half a dozen travel books, with illustrations enhanced by his own accounts of the tour. He kept journals in which he recorded his own observations as well as such things as architectural details. Indeed, his first two volumes of *Illustrated Excursions in Italy,* published in 1846, so appealed to Queen Victoria, that she asked him in that same year to give her drawing lessons.

In London in 1849, he took rooms in Stratford Place suitable for use as living quarters and studio. Years later, in 1857, he lived at 30 Seymour Street, an address that now belongs to the Portman Court Hotel. But inevitably his health would fail and he would flee to the continent, where he continued to suffer from other physical ailments.

Back in England in 1860, he was determined to establish himself as an oil painter. From Holman Hunt, the pre-Raphaelite painter, he had learned that the elements to be included in the composition of a landscape could be found in England; it was not essential to be at the actual source. Thus, when he needed cedar trees for the large canvas he was planning, he was delighted to find the Oatlands Park Hotel with its forty acres of grounds in which stood cedar trees, which are still there today. He expected to work through the winter, and the Oatlands Park Hotel sounded like a good winter residence. He referred to its dry soil, which did not adversely affect his asthma or 'roomatizsim'. Its ideal location, less than twenty miles from central London, made it an accessible place where friends could easily join him. In September 1860 he settled in.

A royal palace had stood on the site which was now a residence for another king—King Lear, as he was called by Millais. Henry VIII built a palace here for his new queen, Anne of Cleves, who probably never actually lived there. Elizabeth I, however, was a frequent visitor to the imposing palace standing in nine acres, and it was a favourite residence of James I. The fourth son of Charles I was born there, and a cedar tree which still stands was supposedly planted to commemorate the event.

The palace was eventually demolished and a house erected on the site where the hotel now stands. Of that mansion with its formal gardens and shell grotto, only prints remain which can be seen in the corridor leading to the dining room. Rebuilt after a fire in 1794, the new house went through several changes of ownership until it was purchased in 1856, remodelled, enlarged with a new west wing and converted into the Oatlands Park Hotel.

Since Lear's stay, the hotel has been further enlarged by a dining room extension in 1927 and a ballroom in 1930. Now, with 145 bedrooms, with all sorts of sports including tennis and golf, and with a superb view all around and down to the River Wey, it functions as a large, old world English country hotel.

In the calm atmosphere of a lovely Sunday afternoon, it gives the impression of a well-kept Hollywood set design or a museum piece. The scenario shows residents seated in the large and comfortable lounge quietly greeting guests who now come in after a slow stroll about the grounds or a long morning sit, with face to sun. Perhaps they pour a sherry from the bottles they have brought with them, for the hotel is unlicensed. Then, gradually, they get up to go into the dining room for the next tranquil activity, Sunday lunch.

In a letter dated 30 September 1860 to his very dear friend

Chichester Fortescue, whom he often playfully addressed as 40sque, Lear described the hotel as, 'a large & sumptuously commodious place . . . with nice broad terrace walks, & a wonderfully lovely view over the river Temms & the surroundiant landskip . . . I have a large light bedroom delightful to behold & wanting for nought.'

While there, he made a nonsense drawing labelled 'Lear feeding "unfortunate birds" at Oatlands Park Hotel, Weybridge.' Meanwhile he also wrote rhymes and decided to offer a new volume for publication.

Lear left the hotel for London at the end of January. But he returned again for a few days after his beloved sister Ann died on 11 March. As for the painting of 'The Cedars', it was finished by the middle of May. He needed funds to cover expenses including those incurred by his stay at the Oatlands Park Hotel, but the painting was not immediately saleable. It was finally purchased by Lady Ashburton in December 1867 for a fraction of the asking price.

Edward Lear's desire to become a respected and sought-after painter blinded him to his ability and popularity as a writer of nonsense. In his letters and in his diary, he hardly alludes to the poems. Yet his landscapes, a constant struggle, nearly died with the man, while his nonsense, so full of originality and subtleties, brought him immortality.

Other 'volumes of stuff' are *Nonsense Songs, Stories, Botany and Alphabets* (1871) and *More Nonsense* (1872). *Laughable Lyrics* appeared in 1877, the fourth and last nonsense book to be published in his lifetime.

Based on the limerick form, his verses were adapted and perfected in his inimitable style:

There was an Old Person of Bangor,
Whose face was distorted with anger,
He tore off his boots, and subsisted on roots,
That borascible person of Bangor.

And:

> There was an Old Person of Philœ,
> Whose conduct was scroobious and wily;
> He rushed up a Palm, when the weather was calm,
> And observed all the ruins of Philœ.

His playfulness with words is evident. Sometimes he coins words which sound absolutely right and become part of the Lear vocabulary. In later works, he refers to the scroobious manners of the old person of Grange and invents a Scroobious Snake for his nonsense alphabet.

The nonsense becomes a vehicle for expressing deep feelings with an emotional quality that is true to life. His people are in contact with or exploited by the 'they'—that gossiping, interfering, unsympathetic, ubiquitous world of anonymous people we all recognise. His characters—the Jumblies, the Dong with the Luminous Nose, the Pobble—all have human feelings. Though they may seem unlikely, though they may have extraordinary experiences, the reader accepts and believes. Humour arises from the incongruities. And when 'runcible' and 'ombliferous' definitely and perfectly modify the nouns they describe and sound so right, children of all ages are delighted.

But many of the poems are simply not *nice* and contain mean or vicious incidents under the amusing tone. Some characters become the unfortunate victims of blunders (the Old Man of Peru is baked by mistake), some are subjected to violence (the Old Person of Buda is smashed with a hammer). There is unhappiness, cruelty, drowning, even suicide (the Old Person of Tartary divided his jugular artery), and one wonders whether the many examples of unwarranted death in those delightful rhymes are altogether suitable for children. If one persists in trying to apply sense to nonsense, one could conclude that they pierce through protective armour:

There was an Old Man of Cape Horn,
Who wished he had never been born;
So he sat on a chair, till he died of despair,
That dolorous Man of Cape Horn.

Lear moved away from sheer nonsense and moved away from England, simply unable to tolerate its damp climate. Like his characters, he was always on the go. The Owl and the Pussy-Cat travel, as does Mr Daddy Long-legs, who sails with Mr Floppy Fly to the great Gromboolian plain. The Jumblies went to sea in a sieve. The Yonghy-Bonghy-Bo travels

With a sad primaeval motion
Towards the sunset isles of Boshen.

When Edward Lear left England in August 1880 he was never to see his homeland again. He died on 29 January 1888, at San Remo on the Italian Riviera.

THOMAS GRAY

at

THE BURNHAM BEECHES HOTEL
GROVE ROAD
BURNHAM
BUCKINGHAMSHIRE

Far from the madding crowd's ignoble strife,
Their sober wishes never learned to stray;
Along the cool sequestered vale of life
They kept the noiseless tenor of their way.

Elegy Written in a Country Churchyard

Thomas Gray's childhood home in London was full of ignoble strife and he was placed far from it when a maternal uncle, Robert Antrobus, who lived at Burnham in Buckinghamshire, took him in.

Born on 26 November 1716, Thomas Gray was the fifth of twelve children and the only one to survive infancy. His long-suffering mother had to contend with the unfortunate marriage she had made. His father had fits of temper and moods of fury when he would attack his wife. Robert Antrobus, an assistant master at Eton College, arranged for the boy of nine to enter the college and thus the young Thomas escaped from the stifling home atmosphere into a landscape of beauty in the Thames Valley.

Thomas Gray enjoyed the beauties, the poetry, the traditions and the history which surrounded him. During those happy years at Eton, he formed intimate friendships with Richard West, Thomas Ashton and Horace Walpole. He appreciated the accessibility of nearby Windsor Castle as well as the statue in the school yard of Eton's founder, King Henry VI, and paid homage in the poem published in 1742, *Ode on a Distant Prospect of Eton College:*

[63]

Ye distant spires, ye antique towers,
  That crown the watery glade,
Where grateful Science still adores
  Her Henry's holy shade;
And ye, that from the stately brow
Of Windsor's heights the expanse below
  Of grove, of lawn, of mead survey,
Whose turf, whose shade, whose flowers among
Wanders the hoary Thames along
  His silver-winding way.

School holidays were spent at his uncle's house at Burnham. It is situated in an area still famous for the forest of glorious beeches which continue to give the area a unique appeal. A letter Gray wrote to Horace Walpole in August 1736 from the house in Burnham describes the scenery all around:

> I have at the distance of half a mile thro' a green Lane, a Forest (the vulgar call it a Common) all my own; at least as good as so, for I spy no human thing in it but myself; it is a little Chaos of Mountains & Precipices . . . such hills as people, who love their Necks as well as I do, may venture to climb, & Crags, that give the eye as much pleasure, as if they were more dangerous: both Vale & Hill is cover'd over with most venerable Beeches, & other very reverend Vegetables, that like most ancient People, are always dreaming out their old Stories to the Winds.

The 'venerable beeches' are still there in the forest known as Burnham Beeches to give pleasure to walkers and nature lovers; and literary pilgrims may easily visualise young Thomas walking in those woods, Virgil in hand.

The house itself gives the appearance of a grand and spacious country estate set in exquisite and extensive grounds. The view of the light green house with white trim from the curving driveway is impressive and inviting.

[64]

Thomas Gray (1716–1771)
and Burnham Beeches Hotel

The original early Georgian house known to Thomas Gray consisted of the central portion with bays on each side of the front door. Extensions were added on at each end in the nineteenth century. In 1966 the historic house was converted into a hotel and enlarged in 1973 to contain fifty-four bedrooms, all with traditional furnishings and all with private bathrooms. But the new wing is at the back and does not interfere with the splendid view of the house which greets the arriving visitor.

Once inside, a friendly bar just to the right of the entrance area is the place for a drink before dinner in the attractive restaurant just to the left. The handsomely-decorated restaurant is enhanced by a framed copy of Gray's famous *Elegy* and by a painting of the author on the wall opposite.

Various rooms such as the Burnham Room and the Georgian Room are used for private functions. There is a Ballroom and a new conference suite with Gray's Bar and a terrace overlooking the grounds.

Conveniently located near London's Heathrow Airport and only twenty odd miles from central London, the hotel offers not only places of interest in the immediate vicinity, but its own forty acres of interesting parkland with such amenities as tennis courts, a croquet lawn and a putting green for its guests.

Indeed its high standard of comfort belies the discomfort felt by young Thomas, as expressed again in a letter of August 1736 to Horace Walpole from this house. He complained that his uncle's dogs '. . . take up every chair in the house, so I'm forced to stand at this present writing, & tho' the Gout forbids him galloping after 'em in the field, yet he continues still to regale his Ears & Nose with their comfortable Noise and Stink.' (Thomas Gray was never fond of animals.)

After Eton, Gray continued his studies at Cambridge, where he eventually became a university professor. He lived the life of a scholarly recluse but returned frequently to the area he knew from his Eton days. A search into the Buckinghamshire haunts of the poet from the beginning of his creative life in

Burnham to his death in Cambridge must necessarily include the nearby Buckinghamshire village of Stoke Poges.

When his father died in 1741, his widowed mother decided to live with her sister and moved to the village of Stoke Poges. Gray made many visits there and did much writing, including his well-known *Elegy*.

His mother died in 1753 and is buried in the Stoke Poges churchyard. His words, inscribed on the tombstone of his devoted and adored mother, describe her as 'the careful tender mother of many children, one of whom alone had the misfortune to survive her.'

Thomas Gray died on 30 July 1771 at the age of fifty-five and is buried by the side of his mother. A monument pays tribute to the creator of one of the best-known poems in the English language who lies among the 'unhonour'd Dead' where 'the curfew tolls the knell of parting day'.

★ ★ ★

W. S. GILBERT

★ ★ ★

at

GRIMS DYKE HOTEL
HARROW WEALD
MIDDLESEX

The song of birds
In ivied towers;
The rippling play
Of waterway;
The lowing herds;
The breath of flowers;
The languid loves
Of turtle doves—
These simple joys are all at hand
Upon thy shores, O Lazyland!

Utopia Limited

The name of Gilbert is inevitably and irrevocably linked with that of Sullivan. The extraordinary Gilbert-and-Sullivan team created supreme and lasting light operas. Sullivan's entrancing music is absolutely right for the lyrics which can hardly be recalled without the accompanying melody. Yet the lyrics written by W. S. Gilbert are characterised by such wit, brilliance, power and precision that he ought to be acknowledged as a first-rate poet in his own right. When Utopia—unlimited—is established, it will present a world in which '. . . Literary Merit meets with proper recognition—As Literary Merit does in England!'

Before they met Arthur Sullivan was a promising composer and William Schwenk Gilbert was a prominent dramatist. The pair were introduced in 1870 when they collaborated on an unsuccessful operetta called *Thespis* and then parted company. Later, Richard D'Oyly Carte, convinced that they were a perfect partnership, and wanting to establish an

[68]

Grims Dyke
Hotel, home of
W S Gilbert
(1836–1911)

English comic opera tradition in a theatre of his own, brought about the joint production of *Trial by Jury* in 1875. This huge success was followed by *The Sorcerer, HMS Pinafore, The Pirates of Penzance*. . . . a total of thirteen operas which found a home at the Savoy Theatre and gave the partners fame and fortune.

It was a magical combination—professionally—but they were never friends. They were dissimilar in background and personality and quarrelled often, sometimes bitterly. Sullivan's music was appreciated by royalty, and he was knighted in 1883. Many bemoaned the waste of his musical talent which stooped to supply background for Gilbert's lyrics. And Sullivan himself, up to his death in 1900, no doubt remained convinced that he was unfaithful to his musical calling.

Gilbert was merely 'the man who writes words for Sullivan,' and his words were often attacked. Notables such as Charles Dodgson (Lewis Carroll, the creator of *Alice in Wonderland*) found it despicable that Gilbert made clergymen seem ridiculous. He objected also to Gilbert's use of profanity: 'I never use a big, big D——'

One newspaper was offended by the gibes in *Iolanthe* but Gilbert acquired enormous popularity as he expressed the foibles of the Victorian age in ingenious lyrics that entertained a large and appreciative audience. The matchless wit of his words continues to amuse vast numbers of people who listen to the still-relevant eccentricities of lawyers, artists, soldiers, politicians, lovers, kings, people—themselves.

> If this young man expresses himself
> in terms too deep for *me*,
> Why, what a very singularly deep young man
> this deep young man must be!

As for pretenders and bores, he

> . . . has got them on his list;
> They really won't be missed.

Who can forget his chorus of police in the *Pirates of Penzance* who sing heroically and repeatedly about going forward into danger, 'to glory, though they die in combat gory,' but who have to be pushed out, for they *don't* go! Or the First Lord of the Admiralty who polished up the handle of the big front door so carefullee that now he is the Ruler of the Queen's Navee?

He could go beyond satire. A good piece of poetry with beautiful imagery is the love song of Strephon and Phyllis:

> All in all since that fond meeting,
>   When, in joy, I woke to find
> Mine the heart within thee beating,
>   Mine the love that heart enshrined!
> Thou the stream and I the willow
>   Thou the sculptor, I the clay,
> Thou the ocean, I the billow,
>   Thou the sunrise, I the day!

Well rewarded for his literary contribution, Gilbert was able to purchase a beautiful home at the edge of London with the proceeds from the vastly successful productions. He acquired Grims Dyke in 1890, and it remained his home for the last twenty years of his life. He and his wife were happy in the large estate built by the eminent Victorian architect, Norman Shaw. In the heart of Harrow's Weald, formerly the hunting ground of royalty, he lived the life of a country gentleman. The Gilberts gave fancy dress dinners, balls and lavish garden parties. He enjoyed dancing and the company of children, and indulged in a favourite pastime of photography. He loved his home with its well-kept and extensive grounds, which included a lake.

At Grims Dyke, with its seemingly limitless utopian possibilities, *Utopia Limited* was written. This penultimate opera of the Gilbert and Sullivan partnership opened at the Savoy Theatre in 1893. The team parted after their next, and last, opera in 1896, the unsuccessful *The Grand Duke.*

Gilbert, at home, continued to write plays. But although both tried, neither Gilbert nor Sullivan achieved any real success on his own. Gilbert lived the life of a country squire and was knighted, finally, in 1907.

On a sunny day in the year 1911, on 29 May, two girls, guests of the Gilberts, were swimming in the lake in the grounds. One called for help, and Gilbert, ignoring his doctor's instructions to avoid cold water, swam to her rescue. She was safely returned to a manageable depth, but the effort was too much for his heart. 'I would like to die upon a summer day in my own garden,' Gilbert had once said, and his wish had been fulfilled. His ashes lie buried in the parish churchyard in Stanmore, not far from Grims Dyke.

He was seventy-five, the last survivor of the successful triumvirate. Sullivan had died at the age of fifty-eight and D'Oyly Carte in 1901 at fifty-six. One cannot help recalling the Yeoman's words:

> What kind of plaint have I,
> Who perish in July?
> I might have had to die,
> Perchance, in June!

Today, his spirit is very much alive and well and singing at the Grims Dyke Country Hotel, with its rural setting in North London. Although it has lost much of its original acreage (but not the lake with its tragic history), it is nevertheless still a country home turned hotel. And it is a friendly place, particularly on Sunday evenings when Gilbert and Sullivan soirées are held.

One enters the foyer, with its plaque of W. S. Gilbert, from a long driveway nearly opposite a pub with the curious name The Case Is Altered. In the reception hall, it becomes obvious that character, and characters, have been retained. The oak-panelled Yeoman Room restaurant has always been the dining room of the house. The adjoining Patience Bar was the library. The Iolanthe Hall has the original vaulted ceiling, minstrels' gallery and carved marble fireplace. (How was the Azalea Room permitted to intrude?) The house has nine bedrooms, and the Gilbert Suite is traditionally furnished with a four-poster bed. A newly-built wing offers an additional forty bedrooms.

And there in the Iolanthe Hall, on Sunday evenings, guests join in the singing of the words of W. S. Gilbert—clever, entertaining, witty words which will never be forgotten. What! Never? Well, hardly ever!

THE SOUTH OF ENGLAND

WILLIAM MAKEPEACE THACKERAY

★ ★ ★

at

THE OLD SHIP HOTEL
KING'S ROAD
BRIGHTON
SUSSEX

Our young bride and bridegroom had chosen
Brighton as the place where they would pass
the first few days after their marriage; and
having engaged apartments at the Ship Inn,
enjoyed themselves there in great comfort and
quietude.

Vanity Fair

'The oldest hotel in Brighton' started life in the sixteenth
century as the small Ship Tavern with an entrance in Ship
Street. Its original and simple name was modified in 1650 to
differentiate it from the New Ship which was built opposite.
The Old Ship was rebuilt and enlarged several times, so that it
now occupies the entire frontage facing the sea between Ship
Street and Black Lion Street. A distinguished history has
accompanied the hotel throughout the centuries.

A succession of owners included the colourful Nicholas
Tettersell. As captain of a trading vessel, Tettersell played his
part in helping King Charles II escape to France after his
defeat in the Battle of Worcester. A copy of a painting by W.
van de Velde of that ship, renamed the *Royal Escape,* hangs in
the Tettersell Bar of the Old Ship Hotel.

In the mid-eighteenth century, when Dr Richard Russell
'invented' and popularised sea bathing, fashionable crowds

William Makepeace
Thackeray (1811–1863)
(drawing by Daniel
Maclise) and The Old
Ship, Brighton, where he
completed the first
numbers of *Vanity Fair*

flocked to Brighton. So successful was the sea-water cure which he prescribed to patients that the poor fishing village of Brighthelmstone was transformed into a popular and fashionable watering place. A character in Jane Austen's *Pride and Prejudice* echoed the sentiments of the throng by suggesting that 'a visit to Brighton comprised every possibility of earthly happiness.'

The *New Brighton Guide* of 1796 singled out the Old Ship as a place 'where the richer visitors resort'. The hotel really came into its own when Brighton became the stylish sea resort selected by the Prince Regent (later to become King George IV) who wanted a villa to accommodate and reflect his own brilliant social life. He built the oriental fantasy known as the Royal Pavilion, which has become a splendid centre for the public and a symbol and cynosure of Brighton. The sensational eccentricities of the exotic palace are still there to be viewed and enjoyed.

The rich and famous arrived to partake of the delights of the resort. Grand social events took place at the Old Ship, such as the Prince Regent's Ball in 1809. On 9 December 1831 Nicolo Paganini gave a dazzling violin recital, and a plaque in the Ballroom commemorates the event. In the literary world, Charles Dickens stayed there in 1841. And William Makepeace Thackeray stayed there in the 1840s while writing parts of *Vanity Fair,* in which he included a description of 'brisk, gay and gaudy' Brighton.

Renovated in 1895, and with a new east wing completed in 1964, the Old Ship Hotel offers splendid views of the popular resort on the English Channel. The huge Victorian white-elephant relic of a bygone era contains the elegant Regency Room and the Ballroom, which was completed in 1767.

Of the 156 bedrooms, Room 242 has been designated the Thackeray Room. Simply but pleasantly furnished, its only relevant feature is a plaque on the wall outlining the facts of Thackeray's visit to the hotel and calling attention to his fondness for Brighton. He was 'born in Calcutta in 1811 . . .' it begins, and expansion on the bare biographical facts would seem to provide material for many novels.

The novelist's mother, Anne Becher, distraught over the loss of her beloved Lieutenant Henry Carmichael-Smyth, was sent to India in the hope that she would recover from a match deemed unsuitable by her family. The scheme worked, for in Calcutta she met and married Richmond Thackeray who had a good position in the service of the East India Company. They became the parents of an only child, William Makepeace Thackeray. Then, one day, Richmond Thackeray invited a new acquaintance home for dinner. What a shocking and painful scene must have ensued when Captain Henry Carmichael-Smyth walked in. The young lovers had been deceived. She was told that her beloved had died suddenly of a fever. He in turn had been presented with his own unopened letters to her (actually intercepted by a disapproving family), returned as proof of her decision to break the engagement. The deception practised by Anne's family ignored future possibilities, for the young man had been promoted and his prospects were more promising. But nothing could now be done, and the captain resumed his duties.

When Richmond Thackeray died in 1815 of a fever, Anne agreed to marry the captain after a decent eighteen-month interval of mourning. Her young son was sent home to England, as was customary with most Anglo-Indian children, for the advantages of climate and schooling. Thackeray never returned to India but he and his stepfather were destined to become good friends. Indeed, Thackeray later used the retired Major Carmichael-Smyth as the prototype for his Colonel Newcome.

In England, the young Thackeray attended school in several places before going to Trinity College, Cambridge. But he left after his second year without taking a degree. Unsure of a career, he tried law, he studied art for a while, then he found his way into journalism.

Thackeray, who loved writing and was always busy with his craft, began to earn his living by contributing free-lance articles to a wide variety of magazines and newspapers such as the prestigious *Morning Chronicle* and *Punch*. Determined to succeed as a writer, he worked hard to establish himself.

In Paris, where he had gone to study art, he met and married Isabella Shawe. Two children were born, but the second died in infancy. After the birth of a third daughter in 1840, Isabella, who had been severely depressed, succumbed to mental illness. Thackeray, busy and preoccupied with his work, failed to recognise the symptoms of his wife's worsening condition. As she continued to sink, he remained determined to rise to the ranks of great writers.

In 1845 he started to write *Vanity Fair*. This was the year in which his wife, whose mental state had been steadily deteriorating, had to be removed from the family. She was never to recover from her incurable illness (although she outlived him by thirty-six years) and he buried himself in his work.

The first number of *Vanity Fair*, which was being published in monthly instalments, appeared in January 1847, and the last in July 1848. With publication of his novel in volume form on 18 July 1848, coincidentally his thirty-seventh birthday, Thackeray was established as one of the leading novelists of the day.

Much of the novel was written when he was living in London, at a variety of addresses, but the first numbers were written when he was living at the Old Ship in Brighton, where he sought seclusion (in the autumn of 1846) in order to work on his novel.

He met Miss Kate Perry, daughter of the former editor of the *Morning Chronicle*, who was staying in Brighton with her brother, and formed a close and lasting friendship with her. Miss Perry gives this recollection of how the famous title first came to Thackeray: 'He told me . . . that, after ransacking his brain for a name for his novel, it came upon him unawares, in the middle of the night, as if a voice had whispered, "Vanity Fair." He said, "I jumped out of bed, and ran three times round my room, uttering as I went, *Vanity Fair, Vanity Fair, Vanity Fair*".'

He was delighted with this title because it gave him a focus, a fair of vanities as a corrupting place, and he described early nineteenth-century society in authentic detail.

The book was a great success and he received the adulation of society. Destined to live a bachelor life, he was caught up in a social whirl: he sought fashionable company and places, ate and drank too much and was frequently ill. He visited Brighton often, both for the society it offered and for recuperative purposes, and he started his next novel, *Pendennis*, in Brighton. *Henry Esmond, The Newcomes*, and other novels followed. He gave lecture tours and visited America.

Thackeray is associated with a number of houses in London, which are marked by the familiar blue plaques. He was fifty-three when he died, on 24 December 1863, less than two years after moving into his new home in Palace Green (now the Israeli Embassy). A bust to his memory is in Westminster Abbey. But Thackerayans will surely want to visit the place where his peregrinations took him for relaxation and creation. The Old Ship in Brighton is where Thackeray found conditions auspicious for producing a novel of the highest quality.

CAPTAIN FREDERICK MARRYAT

at

CHEWTON GLEN HOTEL
NEW MILTON
HAMPSHIRE

He felt happy, as people do who have no cares,
from the fine weather—the deep green of the
verdure chequered by the flowers in bloom,
and the majestic scenery which met his eye on
every side.

The Children of the New Forest

The case of Captain Frederick Marryat at Chewton Glen may
be thought of as that of a minor novelist at a major hotel. The
exquisite country-house hotel is situated on the edge of the
New Forest between Southampton and Bournemouth and is
only two miles from the sea. It is located a mere hundred
miles from London, but the guest is immeasurably further
removed from the cares and concerns of ordinary life.

The origins of the hamlet of Chewton go back to Norman
times, but the present house, known as Chewton Glen, was
built in the early eighteenth century in classic Palladian style.
A new central section was added a century later, and further
renovations were made this century, including the addition of
a new bedroom wing when the house became a hotel in 1962.
Duplex suites in the former coach house now provide additional bedrooms, making a total of fifty-three, a substantial
increase from the original eight.

Most of the coach house suites have a sitting room and
outdoor private patio downstairs; upstairs are a balcony with
view over extensive fields, a luxury bathroom, and a bedroom
built in between original beams. Every effort was exerted to
retain the original beams, walls, rafters, even the bolts, of the

[80]

Chewton Glen Hotel, New Milton, where Captain Frederick Marryat (1792–1848), author of *Mr Midshipman Easy*, frequently stayed with his brother old coach house. One suite has kept the vaulted ceiling intact, a ceiling high enough to permit passage of coaches and horses through the natural entrance between the rafters. With consistent good taste, the horse troughs and baskets which once held hay (and now hold flowers) have been preserved and enhance a lovely setting.

The other amenities of a place which abolishes the standardised sterility, so characteristic of most modern hotels, include an attractive Billiard Room and the unobtrusive Lake Suite for conferences. Luxuriously furnished throughout, and ideally situated in one of the richest areas of England, the hotel has won a succession of awards both for its fine restaurant and for continuing high standards of service.

The hotel is a perfect centre for exploring the former royal hunting preserve of William the Conqueror. The New Forest still offers 'majestic scenery . . . on every side' with wild ponies and deer, stretches of heath, thatched Tudor cottages, quaint old churches and footpaths among ancient oaks and beeches. But why would anyone want to leave a perfect country home set in thirty acres of parkland, a home which offers every comfort from superb French cuisine to heated outdoor swimming pool?

In 1837 George Marryat bought the house, and indentures showing the purchase of the property are displayed in the sun lounge. The house remained Marryat property until 1855. During the 1840s the owner's brother, Captain Frederick Marryat, was a frequent visitor.

Born in London in 1792, Frederick Marryat made a successful and active career for himself in the Royal Navy. His *Code of Signals for the Merchant Service* was published in 1817. He was engaged in the Napoleonic wars and was at St Helena when Napoleon died in 1821. A man of many talents, he made a drawing of Napoleon on his deathbed, which is now exhibited at the National Maritime Museum in Greenwich. Another sketch, a version of Napoleon's head alone, is in the Victoria and Albert Museum. In command of many vessels, with many diverse duties, he hunted smugglers in the English Channel and served in the Burmese War of 1824-26.

Marryat's experiences and adventures became the background for his literary work. Having made a name for himself as a distinguished naval man, he proceeded to make a name for himself as an author. His first novel, *Frank Mildmay*, was published in 1829. A year later, at thirty-eight, Marryat retired from the navy and sailed out into literary waters. The publication of *Peter Simple* in 1834 made him famous. *Jacob Faithful* (1834), *Mr Midshipman Easy* (1836), and *Masterman Ready* (1841) are other familiar titles. Altogether, he completed about seventeen works of fiction as well as other books, essays and pieces of journalism.

Eventually, Marryat settled in at Langham in a corner of Norfolk, where his attempts at farming had disastrous financial results. But he continued to write from his Langham home and from a variety of places—London, Brighton, America.

He is generally seen as a life-at-sea novelist in the tradition of Smollett. He influenced Robert Louis Stevenson, particularly in the writing of such works as *Treasure Island* and *The Master of Ballantrae,* and he greatly impressed Joseph Conrad, who called him 'the enslaver of youth.' Indeed, critics often refer to Marryat as Conrad's precursor in sea fiction.

Visits to Chewton Glen and the New Forest undoubtedly gave Marryat the background material for his final and perhaps most popular novel, *The Children of the New Forest.* The book was published in 1847, a year before his death. Logically, he must have derived inspiration for Arnwood, home of the Royalist family in the novel, from its actual prototype, Arnewood, owned by friends of George Marryat. That thatched house, situated in the nearby village of Sway, and now called Cavalier Cottage, gives the onlooker a view of an existing literary link.

The Chewton Glen Hotel keeps alive the memory of Captain Marryat's presence in the house. Names of his books

[83]

and characters, not numbers, identify the guest rooms. Memorable meals are served in the splendid Marryat Room. In the Marryat Bar hangs a framed letter with his signature. And from the bar, an imbiber might order a mint julep to honour Marryat as 'the first Englishman to write about this famous American drink,' as cited by the United Kingdom Bartenders' Guild.

Afternoon tea may be taken in the friendly atmosphere of the main lounge with its upholstered chairs and couches and polished tables. There the fire extends its warmth on chilly days, and there on view are old prints based on sketches made by Marryat.

If, despite the extensive comforts, the visitor wishes to venture out to explore this part of southern England, excursions to nearby villages can be rationalised as homage to the naval writer. The seafaring town of Lymington has Georgian houses and shops along streets which wind their way down toward a colourful harbour. The historic village of Buckler's Hard contains an interesting Maritime Museum and the Master Builder's House (now a hotel) in which lived Master Shipbuilder Henry Adams.

Virginia Woolf pays tribute to Marryat in her book, *The Captain's Death Bed and Other Essays*. The title essay gives a brief account of Marryat's accomplishments in a life which has remained essentially private. To know him, Virginia Woolf suggests, one must turn to his still highly-readable books.

Perhaps one could enlarge on her suggestion. Although one need not search long for a good excuse to visit a superlative hotel, suppose one arrived there with a supply of Marryat novels—novels which evoke a world of the early nineteenth century and which are still highly regarded, even if they are not regarded as masterpieces. Then an adventure in reading could effectively combine with an adventure in living.

ALFRED, LORD TENNYSON

at

FARRINGFORD
FRESHWATER
ISLE OF WIGHT

. . . All by myself in my own dark garden ground,
Listening now to the tide in its broad-flung, shipwrecking roar,
Now to the scream of a madden'd beach dragg'd down by the wave.

Maud

Perhaps because only islands offer that feeling of complete isolation, perhaps because he had always had a passion for the sea, Tennyson was strongly attracted to the Isle of Wight in answer to his need for privacy and seclusion.

He was forty-four and famous when he came to the Isle of Wight in the summer of 1853 with his wife. Publication in 1850 of his enormously popular *In Memoriam* (a tribute to his dear friend Arthur Hallam, who died in 1833) had established him securely as a poet and led to his appointment, in succession to Wordsworth, as Poet Laureate. Also in that year, he married his long-beloved Emily Sellwood. The times of youthful struggles were over.

The journey to his island haven was a long and arduous one, entailing cross-country travel through Hampshire by train and horse-bus to Lymington, then across the Solent in a rowing boat (missing the steamer seemed inevitable) to Yarmouth and proceeding overland to his destination.

When the couple first saw Farringford, they fell in love with the house at first sight. They had come in search of a secluded house away from London's mad strife, and now they delighted in this attractive Georgian building with its eighteenth-century Gothic-style windows and unsurpassable

[85]

view. They agreed immediately to rent it, with an option to purchase. The Tennysons, with their baby son Hallam, were ensconced by autumn. A second son, Lionel, was born the following year in the house destined to be their home for some forty years.

Located on the Freshwater Peninsula on the western end of the island, Farringford overlooks the sea from its position on a high down which is aptly named High Down. The spacious house, which then contained fifteen rooms, is now the superb three-star Farringford Hotel.

The hotel stands in Bedbury Lane about a mile from the village of Freshwater. In the Freshwater Parish Church are monuments to members of the Tennyson family, including one to Lionel, who died in 1886 on his way home from India, and another to Hallam (Lord Tennyson) who died in 1926, leaving 155 acres of cliff land to the National Trust.

Many of Tennyson's possessions at Farringford have been moved to the Tennyson Museum in Lincoln, for he was born in 1809 in the Lincolnshire village of Somersby. A few pieces of furniture, his writing desk and two chairs, are in the Isle of Wight Museum at Carisbrooke Castle.

Structural changes have been made to the house. The present dining room includes the large room built for parties when the house was enlarged in 1871; the library above had a winding stairway by which the poet could escape if warned of the arrival of unwelcome visitors. Also, the splendid view from the drawing room window northward to the English coast is now partially obscured by growth of trees.

Guests will find all the comforts of a well-appointed hotel. The fifty-six bedrooms have private baths. Three lounges, including a Tennyson lounge, add to the indoor comforts, and a variety of outdoor recreational facilities are available in the grounds—swimming pool, putting green, nine-hole golf course, croquet, tennis and horse riding.

The estate was a constant source of pleasure for the poet. He walked a great deal, and a favourite ramble was along the down overlooking the multicoloured sands of Alum Bay to

Alfred Lord Tennyson
(1809–1892) and his home for
many years, Farringford, Isle of
Wight

the Needles, a group of strangely-shaped rocks projecting from the sea. He worked at such physical chores as mowing the lawn and caring for the farm and garden; he made summer-houses out of rushes; and he built a wooden bridge over the lane leading to the farm. He indulged in astronomy and bird watching, observed nature and the sea. And he wrote.

Maud was published in 1855, the first major poem written at Farringford. In it, he described the horrors of industrial town life where 'the poor are hovell'd and hustled together, each sex like swine' and denounced the evil of the place where 'the spirit of murder works in the very means of life'. *Maud* also contained the spirit of Farringford, 'the house half hid in the gleaming wood' and its surroundings, 'the liquid azure bloom of a crescent of sea'. He immortalised the beauties of his new environment:

A million emeralds break from the ruby-budded lime
In the little grove where I sit—

Despite the poor critical reception, the public did buy the book and thereby enabled Tennyson to buy the spacious house.

The Charge of the Light Brigade came to him while walking on High Down. *The Idylls of the King* was also written at Farringford. Later, with the profits of *Enoch Arden*, he purchased the land between Farringford and the sea to ensure that the view would never be spoiled by building.

His popularity grew steadily. Friends and admirers flocked to this literary mecca. Invited guests included such distinguished notables as Browning, Longfellow, Fitzgerald, Lewis Carroll and Darwin. His neighbour, Julia Cameron, photographed him. Garibaldi, the defender of Italian liberty, planted a tree in front of the house. Sir Arthur Sullivan played at Farringford, and Jenny Lind sang there.

But uninvited visitors, seeking a glimpse of the poet, made life on the island intolerable for Tennyson. They hounded him for a few words or for autographs. They accosted him walking on the downs in his familiar broad-brimmed hat and wide-flowing cloak. They continually intruded on his privacy and infuriated him. One celebrity-seeker even climbed a tree to peer through the window to see the poet at work. Because improvements in all kinds of transportation made the island less remote, it had become an easy target for all kinds of unwelcome tourists and sightseers. No, his marine retreat was no longer a secure haven from curious intruders.

He fled from them, sometimes withdrawing to his study, sometimes withdrawing into himself, but eventually to the mainland. In search of peace, Tennyson acquired, by 1869, a house on another inaccessible site, Aldworth, near Haslemere in Surrey. But he continued to reside at his beloved Farringford for several months each year. On one homeward journey to Farringford, while crossing the Solent by ferry, he composed the poem that his son Hallam considered the peak of all his poetry, *Crossing the Bar:*

> Sunset and evening star,
> And one clear call for me!
> And may there be no moaning of the bar,
> When I put out to sea . . .

The 'bar' might have referred to a sandbank across the mouth of the harbour where the River Lymington enters the Solent. Or it might have referred to the sea barrier that separates the island from the Hampshire coast. Metaphorically of course—and this is the real meaning—it referred to Tennyson's own death. He was in his eighty-first year when he wrote it and he died a few years later, in 1892, at Aldworth.

Easy communication with the island, with ferries and hovercrafts at frequent intervals, now makes it possible for the masses to cross the bar, particularly in the overcrowded summertime, when 'overners' (as mainland people are called) come to enjoy the miles of sandy beaches. But the island enjoys mild winters and is attractive throughout the year.

Famous for its sheer natural beauty, other attractions include the twelfth-century Carisbrooke Castle and the royal Osborne House, built for Queen Victoria when she too evinced a need for privacy.

Tennyson's corner of the island is still a place of pilgrimage, and one can still sense his presence there. The name of High Down has been changed to Tennyson Down, and a thirty-eight-foot-high Tennyson Memorial Cross was erected on it in 1897 to honour the poet. The National Trust preserves the land which still offers exciting walks to the Needles amidst spectacular scenery with views of cliffs and coloured sands across the chalk downlands and out to sea.

The secluded Farringford Hotel still has the garden gate by which Tennyson left to walk on the downs. It also has the wooden bridge built by the poet over the lane which separates the grounds from the farm. Opposite the front of the house stands the Wellingtonia tree planted by Garibaldi, which is now eighty feet high. And in the garden one can still hear the sound of the sea from Freshwater Bay, the same 'shipwrecking roar' that the poet heard well over a century ago.

So it is not too late to accept the 'Invitation to Farringford' that Tennyson himself issued in 1854 in poetic lines (actually to the Reverend F. D. Maurice, godfather to Hallam Tennyson) to come to the Isle of Wight:

> Where, far from noise and smoke of town,
> I watch the twilight falling brown
>   All round a careless-ordered garden
> Close to the ridge of a noble down.

THE WEST COUNTRY

VIRGINIA WOOLF

★ ★ ★

at

TALLAND HOUSE
ST IVES
CORNWALL

'Oh, how beautiful! For the great plateful of
water was before her; the hoary Lighthouse,
distant, austere, in the midst; and on the right,
as far as the eye could see, fading and falling,
in soft low pleats, the green sand dunes with
the wild flowing grasses on them, which
always seemed to be running away into some
noon country, uninhabited of men.

To the Lighthouse

Applying a unique and imaginative use to the fig leaf, St Ia
floated over on it from Ireland to give St Ives its name. She
must be credited also with finding a magnificent spot to come
to, well worth the perilous journey. The parish church, a
large and attractive fifteenth-century granite building,
standing very near the sea, is dedicated to her. The figure of St
Ia is on the roof of the church, together with two other Irish
saints, her brothers: Erc went to St Erth, and Uny to Lelant. In
view of such a tradition of creative power, it seems appropriate
that the district should have been discovered by artists, albeit
artists of a less legendary stature.

Formerly known for pilchards, St Ives is now famous for
pictures. Shops brim over with the products of artists and
craftsmen, who come here in droves. And throngs of tourists
come to buy: from the barefoot and hirsute to the conservative
and elderly, all are equally attracted.

Life still revolves around the harbour, and the old fishing quarter known as Down-a-Long retains its charming atmosphere. Intriguing streets often have names to match— Teetotal Street, Virgin Street and Salubrious Place. Although cargoes of pilchards are no longer the characteristic catch unloaded at the quay, the fresh fish harvest includes all kinds of local fish and shellfish, from lobsters and crabs to turbots and John Dory. Sea-gulls add to the bustling scene as they crowd around the quay, oblivious to the fact that the fishing industry has been superseded by the tourist industry. It makes a pretty picture with fine views out over the Atlantic, the sweep of the bay and the Godrevy Lighthouse.

The area all around is rich in scenery. Just half an hour's walk from the centre of St Ives are wild moors—mysterious gorse-grown wastelands, secret and silent, but full of suggestions of a peopled past, with great monoliths raised by pre-Roman tribes. Prehistoric remains—cromlechs and stone circles—are abundant. Less abundant are railways, telephones and traffic, and other nervous maladies of civilisation. St Ives, over 300 miles from London, is endowed with sheer beauty of setting as well as with a sense of the past.

A spacious residence named Talland House stands high above the harbour. Situated in an acre of grounds with lovely lawns and gardens, waterfalls and rock pools, it is within easy walking distance of the beach, shops, or the labyrinth of streets that form the old part of the town. Known as Talland House Holiday Flats, the impressive white building is comprised of self-contained, comfortably-furnished and well-equipped flats, designed to offer guests all the amenities that enhance the perfect holiday. It also offers opportunities for walking and exploring the surrounding wild moors or the many coastal paths with spectacular cliff views, or for simply enjoying the local scenery, as the view of St Ives Bay and the Godrevy Lighthouse is particularly enchanting.

To this Cornish scene, Sir Leslie Stephen came in 1881. So pleased was he with the flourishing artistic centre situated on the north coast of Cornwall, that he bought Talland House

Virginia Woolf
(1882–1941) Talland
House was the holiday
home of her childhood;
and now accommodates
holiday flats

one year later, in the year of his daughter Virginia's birth. Here, the Stephen family spent their summer holidays every year until 1894. Sir Leslie had been quite a good athlete, and now the ageing writer could content himself with walks across the Cornish moors.

He had married Mrs Herbert Duckworth, a widow with three children, after his first wife (Thackeray's younger daughter) died. Vanessa (born in 1879), Thoby (1880), Virginia (1882) and Adrian (1883) are the children of that union.

Virginia was born into the literary environment of an upper-middle and intellectual class, when Sir Leslie Stephen was fifty years old. A well-known, respected writer and biographer and the noted editor of the *Dictionary of National Biography*, it is perhaps his unhappy posthumous fate to be remembered as the father of Virginia Woolf.

Virginia was born at 22 Hyde Park Gate, Kensington, in a house that is still standing. She grew up in that house, but her happiest childhood memories of those early formative years are associated with the holiday house situated high above the St Ives Bay.

An ancient riddle asks an intriguing question:

As I was going to St Ives
I met a man with seven wives;
Seven wives had seven sacks,
Seven sacks had seven cats,
Seven cats had seven kits.
Kits, cats, sacks and wives—
How many were there going to St Ives?

The riddle's question, applied to Talland House, is incalculable, for the house was teeming with people. It was a large, happy family with eight children, seven servants and innumerable friends and relatives. The life style was casual. The family partook of a variety of pleasurable activities such as boating, fishing, bathing, walking, playing cricket, and even night excursions to trap moths, which Virginia wrote about in her essay, *Reading*. Or they simply enjoyed the landscape. Or they wrote. The importance of the St Ives period on her later life and work—on her writing—cannot be over-emphasised: she discusses the art of writing in her *Diary* (19 December 1938) and recalls that it had been, 'absorbing ever since I was a little creature, scribbling a story in the manner of Hawthorne on the green plush sofa in the drawing room at St Ives while the grown-ups dined.'

At the age of ten, she was already making notes, both mental and written, of St Ives events. She and her brother Thoby put together a hand-written weekly periodical called *The Hyde Park Gate News*. On 11 May 1892 they recorded a projected departure for St Ives as 'a heavenly prospect to the minds of the juveniles who adore St Ives and revel in its numerous delights.' On 12 September 1892 she wrote, 'On Saturday morning Master Hilary Hunt and Master Basil Smith came up to Talland House and asked Master Thoby and Miss Virginia Stephen to accompany them to the light-house as Freeman the boatman said that there was a perfect wind and tide for going there. Master Adrian Stephen was much disappointed at not being allowed to go.' That inci-dent became a crucial element of the plot in the novel that is generally considered her masterpiece, *To the Lighthouse*.

But the happy childhood of Virginia ended with the death of her mother in May 1895. Virginia was overcome with grief and at the age of thirteen, she suffered her first breakdown. The situation was exacerbated by the demands of a distraught father who retreated into the consolation of deep mourning. Sir Leslie, finding the thought of life there without his beloved Julia unbearable, gave up Talland House.

In a sense, Virginia never really left St Ives. Its happy memories and indelible images remained with her always, to be translated into words in her later years. In troubled times she returned to this joyful place of childhood holidays for its beneficial effects and for sustenance. When breakdowns recurred, she was nurtured by Cornish memories and helped considerably by return visits.

Her first return to St Ives occurred in 1905 when she took a summer holiday in Carbis Bay, in what she called (in a letter to Violet Dickenson) 'the divinest view in Europe'. She continues:

It is a strange dream to come back here again. The first night we groped our way up to Talland House in the dark, and just peeped at it from behind the Escalonia hedge. It was a ghostly thing to do: it all looked quite unchanged. Old people meet us and stop and talk to us, and remember us playing on the beach.

However, it is the loveliest country, whatever age you happen to be, and really not spoilt. We went for a walk this afternoon which we used to every Sunday, and saw the Lizard and St Michaels Mount.

And this letter to Emma Vaughan dated 17 September 1905:

Why do you go to Suffolk when you might come here? We have a little lodging house, of the most glaring description, but the divinest country all round. Moors, seas, hills, rocks, a land flowing not only with honey but with cream. Here Nessa paints all the afternoon; and I write all the morning from 10 to 1. Thoby and Adrian discuss points of law; and then take to piquet. We all walk and wander like so many disembodied ghosts. We go to tea with the people who now own Talland. They are a delightful pair of artists, with a family of the age we used to be.

Virginia had continued her practice of writing, as literary exercises, descriptions of the places she visited.

After the death of her dear brother Thoby, she made several visits to Cornwall and wrote one letter of particular interest, to Lady Ottoline Morrell, dated 11 March 1909, 'I wish one could manage so that Bloomsbury was on the sea shore; and all your company sat among seahills.'

In Sussex, she found a semi-detached house at Firle, near Lewes, which she rented and named Little Talland House in what some might call a fixation on her St Ives childhood. She settled in in 1911. From Little Talland House she writes to Clive Bell on 18 April 1911, 'I've found a new walk every day. You must come here and go there with me. There are plains, rivers, downs and the sea to choose from. You will wag your head, and say "Poor creature! Cornwall again!"'

In 1912, at the age of thirty, she married Leonard Woolf, one of the members of the Bloomsbury group. The denigrating name was applied by outsiders to the group of notables who met in the neighbourhood of Bloomsbury to share artistic purposes and friendship. Virginia and her sister Vanessa (who married Clive Bell) had been hostesses in this highbrow Bohemian world. Now Leonard and Virginia Woolf founded the Hogarth Press, and she worked actively toward the success of this publishing venture that produced much fine literature, including her own novels.

It was Cornwall again when she returned with Leonard in April 1914 for a three-week holiday to Lelant, St Ives and Carbis Bay. Overworked and plagued by a series of mental crises, recovery was to be fortified by a return to the West Country. Despite difficulties and frenzied moments, she found succour and a sense of calm in the nostalgic return to childhood scenes. Some years later they went househunting, but Cornwall was too far from London and they ended up buying Monks House in Rodmell, Sussex, on the bank of the River Ouse.

Virginia's first novel, *The Voyage Out*, came out in 1915. While it may show the uncertainties of an insecure novelist, it also shows insights and meaningful commentaries on life in a plot which has the young and motherless Rachel voyage out with her aunt and uncle to a remote spot in South America. Significantly, for her sensitive examination of the voyage out into life, Virginia Woolf is comfortable in a sea setting.

'No casements are so magic, no faery lands so forlorn,' Leonard Woolf philosophises, 'as those which all our lives we treasure in our memory of the summer holidays of our childhood.' The influence and impact of Talland House and its environment continues unabated in the two novels which followed, *Night and Day* (1919) and *Jacob's Room* (1922).

Although *Mrs Dalloway* (1923) is set entirely in London, the city and its characters take on sea symbols and rhythms and colours. Clarissa Dalloway expresses her state of well-being by thinking back to youth: '. . . what a morning—fresh as if issued to children on a beach . . . like the flap of a wave; the kiss of a wave . . .' Thus is Clarissa described in her silver-green dress: 'But age had brushed her; even as a mermaid might behold in her glass the setting sun on some very clear evening over the waves.'

In *To the Lighthouse* the seaside dominates. Preparatory to her great novel, she records in her *Diary* (14 May 1925) her desire to 'get on to *To the Lighthouse*. This is going to be fairly short; to have father's character done complete in it; and mother's; and St Ives; and childhood; and all the usual things I try to put in—life, death, etc.'

Although the fictional aspect places the Ramsay family on a holiday in the Hebrides, the setting is unquestionably Cornwall. Some readers complained that descriptions of the fauna and flora were inaccurate—there are no elm trees in the Hebrides, for instance. Her critics were right, of course, for despite the geographical name Virginia Woolf was describing the magic of Cornwall, the summer home of the Stephen family at St Ives and the Godrevy Lighthouse.

The Godrevy Lighthouse, visible from Talland House, was one of the happy childhood images indelibly etched into her imagination and being:

Indeed they were very close to the Lighthouse now. There it loomed up, stark and straight, glaring, white and black, and one could see the waves breaking in white splinters like smashed glass upon the rocks. One could see lines and creases in the rocks. One could see the windows clearly; a dab of white on one of them, and a little tuft of green on the rock . . . the Lighthouse one had seen across the bay all these years; it was a stark tower on a bare rock.

The Waves (1931) is a poetic novel which is again haunted by sea memories and imagery. Its poetry comes from the powerful images taken from the world she loved: the ocean with its waves, the sky full of birds, driftwood on the shore, cliffs, house and garden—the world of St Ives and Talland House.

She was always in a state of exhaustion and despair in the interval between completion of a book and its publication. The possibility of a crisis was always there. After sending the corrected proofs of *The Waves* to the printer, Leonard records that she was dangerously close to a breakdown. He insisted on a holiday in the hope of finding peace and relief. He describes their visit to the West Country, to 'that strange primordial somnolent Cornish peninsula between Falmouth and Helford Passage, where the names of the villages soothe one by their strangeness—Gweek and Constantine and Mawnan Smith.' They capped the two-week holiday with a visit to St Ives and Talland House, where Virginia peered through the ground floor windows at the ghosts of her childhood. Naturally, she was also driven to write another novel.

After *The Years* (1937) was published, she asked in her *Diary*, in characteristic imagery, 'Will another novel ever swim up?'

Virginia Woolf, whose concern with the flow of time in her novels and with continual change, used the flow of water to represent the flux of life. Her power transferred the vision to pages of books. Her own life ended (in 1941) with her being absorbed into the flowing waters of the River Ouse.

'Then the curtain rose' is the concluding line of her posthumous novel, *Between the Acts*. The vicissitudes of life go on. Events, like waves from the sea, keep occurring. One play, one bit of action, is ending, but another has already formed and is beginning to follow its inexorable course. For Virginia Woolf, the curtain rose in Cornwall.

DYLAN THOMAS

at

THE LOBSTER POT
MOUSEHOLE
CORNWALL

> Polgigga is a tiny place two miles or less from
> Land's End and very near Penzance and
> Mousehole (really the loveliest village in
> England).
>
> Letter to Vernon Watkins 20 April 1936

Granted that Dylan Thomas was given to exaggeration, his Mousehole accolade—the loveliest village in England—is nevertheless not inaccurate. Like Laugharne, the Welsh village with which he is generally associated, Mousehole (pronounced Mou´ zl) is a poet's place. It is a pretty fishing port which looks out to the sea over a snug and secure harbour draped with the nets of fishermen who crowd the village. The picturesque village is crowded too with holiday visitors, and the narrow streets become clogged with traffic in the busy summer season.

Once important enough to have been an embarkation port for pilgrims sailing to the Holy Land, and in the fourteenth century the most important fishing harbour in West Cornwall, Mousehole appeals to sightseeing visitors. Meandering through the winding lanes and alleys, perhaps while munching on a Cornish pasty, is an enjoyable pastime which reveals picture-postcard cottages built of local granite and slate—a photographer's dream. A private home called Keigwin Manor has been restored to look like the Elizabethan house which was destroyed when the Spaniards burnt the village in 1595 as a reprisal after the defeat of the Armada. The Ship is one inviting pub, and the Lobster Pot is a genuinely old and charming hotel, a leading attraction of Mousehole. The Lobster Pot is believed to have been built around 1595. The rambling inn is made up of adjoining fishermen's cottages and has twenty-four bedrooms, many with sea views which are a treat. The marvellous meals, served in its justifiably famous restaurant overhanging the harbour, feature lobsters, crayfish, crabs and oysters from the sea just outside. With gulls perched on the steeply-pitched slate roofs, the cosy inn has an evocative atmosphere. Everything conspires to give the feeling of an ancient fishing village, perhaps used as the setting for a fanciful story in a book of old tales.

Although the actual story of Dylan Marlais Thomas begins and ends in Wales, Cornwall is a place of special significance for the Welsh national poet; it was in Cornwall that he and Caitlin Macnamara were married, and there they spent their honeymoon. Dylan was born in Swansea on 27 October 1914. He left at the age of twenty in order to pursue his craft or sullen art in London but returned to Wales after his marriage, to live in Laugharne. After he died in New York City, on 9 November 1953, while on a lecture tour in the United States, his body was brought back for burial in St Martin's churchyard in Laugharne.

Dylan Thomas first met Caitlin Macnamara in London in April 1936. Caitlin was a very pretty girl of twenty-three, given to eccentric dress and behaviour. She had run away to London in pursuit of a career on the stage and was involved with the art of dancing, which she was learning to do in the Isadora Duncan style. Dylan had come to London to work and to see his publisher about his forthcoming second volume of poems. The couple were introduced in a London pub by Augustus John of the large John family with whom the Macnamara children had grown up.

Shortly after their magical meeting, Caitlin and Dylan parted. She returned to her home in Hampshire where her portrait was being painted by Augustus John. Dylan left for Cornwall, for he had accepted an invitation from Wyn Henderson to her Cornish retreat, a cottage at Polgigga,

Dylan Thomas
(1914–1953) and The
Lobster Pot,
Mousehole, where he
and Caitlin spent their
honeymoon

between Penzance and Land's End. Mrs Henderson, a capable and understanding person with a special position among an artistic group, had been involved in writing and publishing and was to run Peggy Guggenheim's Bloomsbury art gallery. In Cornwall, Dylan did a lot of drinking and a little bit of writing and was well cared for by Wyn Henderson.

By June 1937, Dylan and Caitlin decided to get married in what he calls in a letter to his parents a 'rash and mad scheme'. He had fallen in love at the first meeting and remained in love (despite altercations and infidelities) throughout the seventeen years of his remaining life.

In the spring, he and Caitlin had gone down to Cornwall, staying in a borrowed cottage in Lamorna Cove. Wyn Henderson was by then running a guest house called the Lobster Pot, on Mousehole Harbour, in partnership with Max Chapman. The young couple moved to the Lobster Pot and were married on 11 July 1937, in the Penzance Registry Office. Dylan was destitute, as usual, and Wyn Henderson paid for the marriage licence. In a letter from the Lobster Pot to his friend Vernon Watkins, dated 15 July 1937, he wrote, 'My own news is very big and simple. I was married three days ago; to Caitlin Macnamara; in Penzance registry office; with no money, no prospect of money, no attendant friends or relatives, and in complete happiness. We've been meaning to from the first day we met, and now we are free and glad.'

They spent their honeymoon at the Lobster Pot, then moved to the nearby fishing village of Newlyn to a studio owned by Max Chapman. They associated with painters and writers staying in the area, which had become something of an artists' colony, and a good time was had by all. At the end of the summer they left Cornwall to visit his parents in Swansea.

From the creative point of view little happened in 1937, but Dylan Thomas did write a long poem originally entitled *Poem to Caitlin*, then *Poem (for Caitlin)* and later known by its first line, 'I make this in a warring absence.' The 'warring absence' refers to coldness or actual separation from one another:

I make this in a warring absence when
Each ancient, stone-necked minute of love's season
Harbours my anchored tongue, slips the quaystone,
When, praise is blessed, her pride in mast and fountain
Sailed and set dazzling by the handshaped ocean,
In that proud sailing tree . . .

This long, difficult and obscure poem uses the sea and
harbour images which were all around at the time of writing.
The absence prevents speech, and the tongue, inactive, is like
a ship tied up in the harbour. The imagery reflects Cornwall.

Despite a diminished fishing fleet and despite a throng of
summer holiday makers, it is still possible to find sandy
beaches and peaceful coves in an area whose very name is
enchanting. It is easy to dredge up romantic images of the
caves where pirates and smugglers once hid contraband
goods. In this idyllic place in which pressures of time and
work are dispelled, it seems so right to invoke the poetic past
and recall one of the world's great poets—Dylan Thomas.

━━━━━━━━━━━━━━━━━ ★ ★ ★ ━━━━━━━━━━━━━━━━━

KATHERINE MANSFIELD

━━━━━━━━━━━━━━━━ ★ ★ ★ ━━━━━━━━━━━━━━━━━

at

HANNAFORE POINT HOTEL
MARINE DRIVE
WEST LOOE
CORNWALL

> We drove through lanes like great flowery
> loops with the sea below and huge gulls
> sailing over or preening themselves upon the
> roof tiles, until we came to this hotel which
> stands in its garden facing the open sea. It
> could not be a more enchanting position. The
> hotel is large, 'utterly first class,' *dreadfully
> expensive.* It has a glassed-in winter garden for
> bad weather with long chairs, a verandah—the
> garden hung between the sun and the sea.

Letter to John Middleton Murry 17 May 1918

When it was known as the Headland Hotel, Katherine
Mansfield came to it to recover from her illness. Set on the
glorious Cornish coastline in an area of great natural beauty,
the hotel is a perfect haven for health and for happiness. Alas,
Katherine Mansfield found neither.

She first came to England in 1903 to complete her education
at Queen's College in London. Upon returning to New
Zealand, where she was born on 14 October 1888, she found the
atmosphere narrow and stifling and begged to be allowed to
return to London. At last her parents yielded, and the twenty-
year-old girl left the place of her birth never to return.

In London she entered a bohemian world and she entered a
marriage which she left the very next day. She had succumbed
to the persuasive charms of the man whom she married when
she found herself pregnant and rejected by another. But her
marital motive, an impulsive bid for security, had a

[106]

Katherine Mansfield
(1888–1923) Headlands
Hotel, now Hannafore
Point Hotel, West Looe,
where she wrote her story
Carnation

predictably unhappy ending. She left her husband and the world of promising bourgeois possibilities. In Bavaria shortly thereafter, where she was so intolerably miserable that she relied on drugs for relief, she suffered a miscarriage. Her first book contained the cynical stories emanating from that dreadful time in her life; *In a German Pension*, published in 1911, expresses the feelings of an outsider in a hostile world.

A complex person who donned many masks and roles, Katherine Mansfield continued to have love affairs. On her return to London, there was a second pregnancy and an abortion. She seemed always to be seeking intensive experiences from which she might shape the stories which would bring her closer to becoming the well-known and creative writer she had long before determined to be.

She first met John Middleton Murry in 1911 after he wrote to her asking her to send a story to the Oxford undergraduate magazine of which he was editor. Her story appeared in *Rhythm* in the spring issue of 1912. Katherine and Murry became good friends. By Easter he moved into her flat, and they both worked on the quarterly magazine which included stories, essays and reviews by Murry and Katherine and their friends.

Finally, she no longer felt isolated and lonely—no longer an alien. She could share life with someone she loved, someone who was also her critic and confidant. They married on 3 May 1918, a few days after she obtained a divorce ending that first disastrous marriage.

But the chance for marital happiness was marred by the onset of tuberculosis. Although happy in London with her husband, her health steadily declined. Illness made it essential for her to leave England every winter. She had spent one winter in the milder climate of the south of France but returned to England in even poorer health than before she left. Frequent separations from Murry and worries over financial problems no doubt contributed a deleterious effect to her physical condition.

Murry was unable to convince her to enter a sanatorium but

he was able to convince her to go to Cornwall. After only a few weeks of marriage, in the middle of May, she went to the luxurious Headland Hotel in Looe, recommended by a friend. A letter dated 19 May 1918, to Murry, underscores the ironies and contingencies of life: '. . . the divine sea is here, the haze and brightness mingled. I stare at that and wonder about the gulls, and wonder why I must be ill.'

She also expresses anxiety, in letters to Murry, about the acceptance of *Bliss*. One of her best-known short stories, *Bliss* was written at a time of illness and wretchedness. The story deals with the familiar theme of the heroine's happiness so suddenly and unjustly demolished. The young woman of the story feels the beauty of a spring day with the pear tree in full bloom in the garden. In a state of bliss, she senses something wonderful about to happen. But her hopes are cruelly destroy-ed, while nature remains untouched by her tragedy: 'But the pear tree was as lovely as ever and as full of flower and as still.'

It should have been a happy stay in Cornwall. Indeed her letters from Looe were cheerful enough at first, as in this of 1 June 1918, to Murry: 'I've not moved from my balcony all day. If you could see the water, half green half a tender violet, and just moving. It is unbelievably exquisite.'

But when overwhelming depression took over, the world became ugly. In a letter to Lady Ottoline Morrell she writes, 'the sea stank—great gray crabs scuttled over the rocks—all the private paths and nooks had been fouled by human cattle —there were rags of newspaper in the hedges. . . .'

She was especially taken with an angel of a chambermaid, Mrs Honey, who was completely devoted to her. A letter of 18 May 1918 to Murry playfully describes the maid: 'The old woman who looks after me is about 106, nimble and small, with the loveliest *skin*—pink rubbed over cream—and she has blue eyes and white hair and *one tooth*, a sort of family monument to all the 31 departed ones. Her soft Cornish cream voice is a delight . . .' Mrs. Honey was actually sixty-eight and full of tender care and concern for Katherine. Despite good care, Katherine entered this wry description of a sleepless night in her journal. 'The man in the room next to mine has the same complaint as I. When I wake in the night I hear him turning. And then he coughs. And I cough. And after a silence I cough. And he coughs again. This goes on for a long time. Until I feel we are like two roosters calling each other at false dawn. From far-away hidden farms.'

Despite the sea and sun, she became disillusioned. Her initial contentment turned to bitterness and despair. She missed Murry and was in constant pain, clinging desperately to love and life. A projected stay of three months was reduced to five weeks. Murry came down to bring her home in the third week of June. They had found in Hampstead the house which they called 'The Elephant' (now marked by a blue plaque) and were able to move into it at the end of August. Also in August of 1918, *Bliss* was published in the prestigious *English Review*.

Very little writing survives of Katherine Mansfield's stay in Cornwall. Part she destroyed herself, part was lost—a journal of her observations. There is the complete story *Carnation* plus a few fragmentary pieces.

But after her stay in Cornwall, Katherine Mansfield began a period of intensive writing, and many of her mature stories present a world of beauty suddenly shattered by the inexplicable and capricious entry of evil into a world indifferent to human suffering. When she was not feeling debilitated by disease, her feverish application to work during the final years resulted in artistic triumph over physical disability.

In 1920 the volume *Bliss and Other Stories* was published and in 1922 *The Garden-Party and Other Stories*. She was now financially secure and famous. Her reputation remains untarnished as critics continue to appreciate and respect her enormous influence on the art of the short story.

Katherine and Murry returned to London to live, but she kept going abroad for health reasons—the Italian Riviera, the French Riviera, Switzerland, Paris. She resumed the journey of the consumptive seeking health, the journey made by Keats, Chekhov and Lawrence. She moved about from place to place in search of a cure and underwent quack treatments, radiation therapy and, finally, even a kind of mystical or faith healing. After five years of illness and suffering, her premature death at the age of thirty-four came in France on 9 January 1923.

But the world of beauty in which the hotel exists remains unchanged. The name of the hotel is changed—but not the qualities which make it special. The Headland Hotel became the Hannafore Point Hotel in the 1950s, but its venue remains altogether joyous in its 'enchanting position'.

The hotel has forty bedrooms all with private bathrooms and many with balconies overlooking Looe Bay. An outdoor swimming pool has also been added. But most important is 'all that sea and air outside' which Katherine Mansfield speaks of in her letters and in her journal. In a letter to Lady Ottoline Morrell of 24 May 1918, she tries to banish despair and fits of weeping, 'My tiny world tinkles: "Of course, with all that sea and air outside and all that butter, milk and cream *in* you'll be as fit as a fiddle in no time".'

When she was feeling well enough to go out, she did get about and responded with pleasure and vigour to her surroundings. She describes to Virginia Woolf the little town of Looe 'built on both banks of a deep river and joined by an extremely "paintable" bridge. And seagulls, and flowers— and *so on.*'

East Looe and West Looe are joined by an attractive Victorian bridge, erected to replace the earlier fifteenth-century bridge of thirteen arches. The hotel is in West Looe, but the main part of the village clusters around the quay. In one of the appealing old streets of East Looe is a sixteenth-century guildhall, now a museum.

Katherine Mansfield describes the nearby picturesque fishing village of Polperro with its 'lovely little black and white and grey houses—houses that might have been built *by* sea-gulls *for* sea-gulls. But you must see this yourself. You'll *not* believe it. I didn't, and can't even now. It was a divine afternoon, foxgloves everywhere, AND we found the most

SUPERB fresh strawberries.' It is still a charming village with fascinating streets. Around the harbour, simple colour-washed Georgian houses are reflected in the water. A long history of smuggling activity makes it even more colourful, and a smuggler's museum is located in the cellar of a house near the centre of the village.

Nowadays, the area around Looe boasts of such unusual attractions as an organ museum and a monkey sanctuary as well as the usual attractions of golf, boating and sea bathing. But the unchanging aspect of the area includes ancient stone circles and simply gorgeous scenery.

Katherine Mansfield's description of an 'ideal beach, really ideal . . .' might make anyone dash off to explore the Cornish area: 'This is the most astounding place. Where we were was absolutely deserted—it might have been an island—and just behind us there were great woods and fields . . .'

But perhaps the last word for visiting Looe with its timeless sense of the past, including Katherine Mansfield's presence, can best be left to her lyrical and evocative description from this journal entry of 22 May 1918. 'The sea here is real sea. It rises and falls with a loud noise, has a long, silky roll on it as though it purred, seems sometimes to climb half up into the sky and you see the sail boats perched upon clouds—like flying cherubs.'

at

GREENBANK HOTEL
HARBOURSIDE
FALMOUTH
CORNWALL

He marched into the inn, ordered the best
luncheon that could be provided at so short a
notice, and sat down to eat it in the coffee-room.

The Wind in the Willows

When Kenneth Grahame wrote the famous children's classic
which has gone into over a hundred editions since its
publication in 1908, he had already achieved fame as a writer.
He had created an idealised picture of childhood in *The
Golden Age* and *Dream Days,* both extremely popular. A
more unlikely candidate for the author of *The Wind in the
Willows* would be hard to visualise.

He was born in Edinburgh on 8 March 1859. His mother
died when he was five, and the four Grahame children were
sent by their father to live with their maternal grandmother at
Cookham Dene in Berkshire. He developed a love of nature
and a love for the Berkshire portion of the River Thames,
which he used as the home of his animal characters. Years
later, after a career in London, Grahame was to return to
Cookham Dene with his wife and son. Like his own character
Mole, a mysterious call reached him. 'Home! That was what
they meant, those caressing appeals, those soft touches
wafted through the air, those invisible little hands pulling
and tugging, all one way!'

Not permitted to go to Oxford, the young Grahame entered
into a clerkship in the Bank of England on the first day of 1879.

The condemned man resented all his life the denial of a university education and the career decision which was made for him. But he stayed with the Old Lady of Threadneedle Street for nearly thirty years and found solace in holidays, both in England and abroad; in particular he discovered and fell in love with Cornwall, returning to it often.

He was making a success of life. He advanced in his career, and he wrote essays, a selection of which were published as *Pagan Papers* in 1893. He may even be credited as an early feminist writer for his single adult short story, *The Headswoman* (which appeared in *The Yellow Book* in 1894). Written at a time of controversy over the employment of women at the Bank, this satirical story was about a woman claiming her rights to a hereditary position as executioner in a sixteenth-century French village. But *The Golden Age* (1895), a collection of eighteen articles about children, made him famous overnight.

The year 1898 was a highly successful one in both his professional and literary life. At the age of thirty-nine, he became Secretary of the Bank of England. And *Dream Days* was published in December to enthusiastic reviews. Now he was a financially secure and highly eligible bachelor of nearly forty. His housekeeper, in his quarters in Kensington Crescent, conceived of him as a Mr Jekyll who went to the Bank of England and Mr Hyde 'who wrote bits in the papers.'

Indeed, the idea of a person serving in the Bank conjures up a picture of a stodgy man in formal attire, with black umbrella and silk top hat, stiff and uncomfortable with children—an image of solid respectability. A colleague at the Bank purchased *The Golden Age* believing it to be about bullion or currency. Both the colleague and the image were wrong.

Elspeth Thomson entered his life in 1897, and the friendship culminated in marriage. She came down to Fowey in Cornwall when he was convalescing from an illness, and they were married there on 22 July 1899. Unfortunately, it was to be a disappointing and unhappy marriage for both partners.

Their only child was born on 12 May 1900. He was blind in

Kenneth Grahame (1859–1932)
and The Greenbank Hotel,
Falmouth, from where he wrote
letters containing the adventures of
Toad to his son

one eye with a squint in the other, and he was destined to be spoilt, unhappy, and unable to live up to the level of expectations set for him. His father's repressed imagination and creative impulses found release by focussing on Alistair— 'Mouse' as their young son was affectionately called.

The Wind in the Willows evolved from the bedtime stories Kenneth Grahame told his son over a three-year period, beginning in early 1904. He writes in a letter of 15 May 1904 that Alistair had a fit of crying, '. . . and I had to tell him stories about moles, giraffes & water-rats till after 12.' In that same month, the maid, asked by Elspeth why the master was late when they were going out to dinner, replied, 'Oh, he's up in the night-nursery, telling Master Mouse some ditty or another about a toad.'

While the giraffe was dropped from the cast of characters, a guest shamelessly eavesdropping in rapt fascination to the story Grahame was telling Alistair, reported in August 1905 that a badger had been added.

In May 1907, Alistair was sent to Littlehampton with his governess on a seven-week seaside holiday. To placate the child, his father promised to send letters containing the continuing saga of the adventures of the toad so that Mouse would not miss the bedtime stories. While the child was enjoying the sea and sand, his parents left for Cornwall. They spent some ten days at the Greenbank Hotel in Falmouth before going on to Fowey. Then Elspeth returned in mid-June to be with Alistair, who was now back at home in Cookham Dene, but Grahame (for some inexplicable reason) stayed at their London pied à terre until September, returning to Cookham Dene for weekends.

It is during the period of time from the spring to the autumn of 1907 that Kenneth Grahame wrote the letters which the governess read to Alistair at bedtime. Fortunately, she also preserved them, for they contained the basic narrative of Toad's adventures. A letter of 10 May from the Greenbank Hotel begins, 'Have you heard about the Toad?' and ends, 'I fear he is a bad, low animal.'

When *The Wind in the Willows* was published, not many people realised what a strong and lasting wind blew. The book had a slow and indifferent reception and was initially appreciated by few. Arnold Bennett reviewed it and pointed out its value, speaking of its characters—the Rat, the Mole, the Toad—as human beings. Toad does have the appeal of the ever-popular bad boy, wild and boastful, but full of spirit and fully confident of finding a way out of his predicament.

The story is set mainly in the geographical area of the Thames from Marlow to Pangbourne, especially around Cookham Dene. Grahame knew the area as a child and returned to it in middle age for his escape into an ideal social world. By drawing on actual memories for some of his descriptions, he gave a powerful feeling of reality. 'As you went along in the stillness, every now and then masses of snow slid off the branches suddenly with a *flop!* making you jump and run for cover.'

In a letter dated 10 October 1908 to one of his many enthusiastic fans, President Theodore Roosevelt, he wrote of *The Wind in the Willows:* 'Its qualities, if any, are mostly negative—i.e., no problems, no sex, no second meaning—it is only an expression of the very simplest joys of life as lived by the simplest beings of a class that you are specially familiar with and will not understand.' This effacing statement is denied by critics who find significant, latent meanings as they delve into the characters of Grahame's private world. Although he displayed outward conformity to society, inwardly he found revenge in satire and fantasy. He found relief in a world of childhood.

Kenneth Grahame retired prematurely from the Bank in June 1908. He did a great deal of travelling but never went to the United States. He never accepted the invitation extended by Theodore Roosevelt to visit him at the White House, but the two met when Roosevelt came to Oxford to lecture several years later. In his travels, Cornwall always remained a special haven. 'I want Mouse to make the acquaintance of my Cornish haunts, and friends,' he wrote, 'before he goes to school.'

[117]

Alistair's days at school were sheer misery. He was semi-blind, awkward, and friendless and went from one emotional crisis to another. He continued to be unhappy at Oxford when he went up to Christ Church in the spring term of 1918. Then on 7 May 1920 tragedy struck. Out on an evening walk by himself, while crossing railway tracks, he was killed by an oncoming train. Although a coroner's jury returned a verdict of accidental death, doubts remain. (Why did he indulge in an unaccustomed glass of port before going out? Aware that his vision was poor, why did he not choose the proper crossing instead of a spot some distance from it? Even if he could not see well, could he not *hear* the train approaching?) In any case, the recipient of those comforting bedtime tales was dead at twenty.

The Grahames made their last home at Church Cottage, Pangbourne, in the Berkshire countryside which Kenneth loved. He wrote a little, travelled, and lived out his final years quietly. He died on 6 July 1932.

The world he created continues to enchant, as does the actual world in which he lived, a world which goes through the Berkshire landscape on to Cornwall. As Rat expresses it, 'Beyond the Wild Wood comes the Wide World.'

And in the wide world is Falmouth, a lovely seaport with a climate so mild that oranges and bananas have been grown, and tropical plants thrive in public gardens. And at the mouth of the Penryn River is the Greenbank Hotel, looking across the harbour towards St Mawes. Henry VIII built castles at Falmouth and at St Mawes to guard the entrance of the estuary from possible attack; they are perhaps among the best preserved Tudor castles in the land.

History and romance conspire at the Greenbank Hotel as it overlooks the harbour from which packet ships and tea clippers once sailed across vast oceans to achieve fame and fortune. The names of those ships and their captains are on the doors of each of the forty comfortable guest rooms, many with spectacular waterfront views.

The hotel itself has a long history, for the original building dates from at least 1640. It was a private residence before becoming the Ship Inn and later the King's Arms Inn. Thomas Selley became its proprietor in June 1813 and renamed his establishment the Green Bank, making it a gentlemen's residence where packet captains stayed. In 1869 it came into the hands of the Mitchell family, after whom the present dining room is named.

In the nineteenth century, the Greenbank Hotel was an important stop for coaches leaving for Plymouth, Exeter, London, Bath, and Bristol. Still in the nineteenth century, another well-known visitor stayed here—Florence Nightingale.

The public rooms—two lovely lounges and two bars—display collections of seafaring memorabilia: models of ships, prints and early photographs. It is only appropriate that nautical associations dominate, but the literary association is not neglected. In the reception area are the framed letters written by Kenneth Grahame which form the basis for *The Wind in the Willows*.

From the Greenbank Hotel, the guest can look out at the vista and wonder, as did Rat, 'What seas lay beyond, green, leaping, and crested! What sun-bathed coasts, along which the white villas glittered against the olive woods! What quiet harbours, thronged with gallant shipping bound for purple islands of wine and spice, islands set low in languorous waters!'

at

HOTEL REGINA

TORQUAY

DEVON

My lonely chamber next the sea,
Is full of many flowers set free
  By summer's earliest duty;
Dear friends upon the garden-walk
Might stop amid their fondest talk,
  To pull the least in beauty.

A Flower in a Letter (1839)

Torquay, the large and flourishing seaside resort on the southern Devonshire coast, is a place of palm trees and sub-tropical vegetation. With a very mild climate, a superb panoramic setting, and a variety of holiday attractions, it has won the accolade as the French Riviera of England. Yet Torquay is also the scene of what were undoubtedly the unhappiest years in the life of Elizabeth Barrett Browning.

Elizabeth was born on 6 March 1806, at Coxhoe Hall in the county of Durham. Three years later, after a son and another daughter were born to Edward and Mary Moulton Barrett, the family moved to Hope End. That house (now the site of the Hope End Country House Hotel), near the delightful market town of Ledbury in Herefordshire, is the home of Elizabeth's childhood and youth, and the place where literary foundations and aspirations were laid. It is also the place where the family greatly increased in size, with the birth of two more daughters and seven more sons and the place where the first attack occurred of the long and serious illness which plagued Elizabeth throughout her life.

Despite her illness and despite the unexpected death of her

Elizabeth Barrett Browning (1806–1861) and Hotel Regina, formerly 1 Beacon Terrace, Torquay, where she lived for two years before her elopement mother, when Elizabeth was twenty-two, the Hope End period was essentially a happy one. But severe financial setbacks forced the family to relinquish a comfortable life style and to give up the paradisiacal setting in the Malvern Hills. Hope End was sold in 1832.

The Barretts lived in Sidmouth in Devon for nearly three years before taking up residence in London, where they rented a house in Gloucester Place. Then Mr Edward Barrett found the house he wanted—50 Wimpole Street—*the* house associated with Elizabeth. The Barrett family moved into it in the spring of 1838. In London, Elizabeth's frail health broke down and her invalidism dates from that time. Confined largely to her room, she wrote incessantly, and the result was the publication of *The Seraphim, and Other Poems*, a volume which firmly established her literary reputation.

When doctors advised a warmer climate for the winter, Torquay was chosen in the hope that the sea air would restore her strength. She left unhappily and unwillingly, sentenced by an illness so serious that she might never return. Her favourite brother Edward, affectionately nicknamed 'Bro', accompanied her in the autumn of 1838, and various members of the family joined her from time to time.

At first they lived in the northern part of Torquay with an aunt and uncle. Then she moved to 3 Beacon Terrace, the warmest situation in the town, with an ideal location which she describes in a letter of October 1838 to Mary Mitford:

Here, we are immediately *upon* the lovely bay—a few paces dividing our door from its waves—and nothing but the 'sweet south' and congenial west wind can reach us—and *they* must first soften their footsteps upon the waters. Behind us—so close as to darken the back windows—rises an abrupt rock crowned with the slant woods of Beacon Hill—and thus though the North and East wind blow their fiercest, we are in an awful silence and only guess at their doings.

[122]

But Number 1 Beacon Terrace offered an even warmer residence, as she reveals in a letter of 30 October 1839, and she again moved. 'The new house is warm and in all ways or *most,* superior to the last.' That house, now the Hotel Regina, is where she lived for two years.

The name of the hotel has undergone several changes since the first baths in Torquay were installed in 1817. The building was then given its original and appropriate name of Bath House. Indeed, excavations made in 1929 to install a lift uncovered some of the old baths underneath the drawing room. After 1857, it was known as Victoria House, later as Sea Lawn, and finally as the Hotel Regina. It had everything going for it then, as now.

The Hotel Regina sounds queenly enough and does command a royal position on the road which runs alongside the seafront on the English Channel. But the unpretentious little place has been renovated recently, modernised and enlarged to suit the needs of the growing clientele which fills the house, especially in the overcrowded summer months. Now the hotel contains seventy-six rooms, most with private bathrooms, and it emphasises the presence of the poetess by a Browning Bar embellished with pictures of Elizabeth Barrett Browning.

Pleasure craft fill the busy harbour, and an attractive scene offers many summer activities as well as a warm winter haven. But for Elizabeth Barrett, 'the lovely bay' became 'this dreadful place'. Illness and tragedy marred the offerings of an ever popular seaside resort.

In Torquay, she remained in a state of poor health, nearly always bedridden in a room facing the bay. Although her health seemed at first to improve, she suffered a relapse in January 1839, followed by partial recovery in the spring. Her up-and-down curve ended in a relapse and serious illness for the rest of her stay in Torquay. Confined to bed in a state of feeble health, her letters often express the hope of leaving. The poems written during this period of ignominious exile indicate her unhappy outlook rather than enjoyment or inspiration derived from an attractive seaside location. In *The Cry of the Human*, one of the short poems written at Torquay, she speaks of 'the tempest . . . the plague . . . the curse . . . the corpse . . . terrors':

The city's golden spire it was,
    When hope and health were strongest,
But now it is the churchyard grass,
    We look upon the longest.

News of the death of her brother Sam in Jamaica in February 1840 caused a near-total collapse. Then came the tragedy from which she never recovered, the death of her beloved brother Edward, drowned in a boating accident on 11 July 1840. He was on a sailing expedition with friends when a sudden squall caused the boat to capsize in Babbacombe Bay. The bodies were discovered washed ashore days later and buried in Tor Churchyard in Torquay. The effect on Elizabeth was disastrous. Grief was exacerbated by guilt. She loved him deeply, and he was in Torquay because of her.

She was left prostrate by the tragedy. When she finally rallied and regained a will to live, she lived only to be released from incarceration in Torquay with its dark associations. But she was simply too unwell to undertake the journey.

In a letter of 12 June 1841, to Richard Horne, she expresses her intense need to go home and speaks of the patent carriage 'with a thousand springs' that will carry her to London, to Wimpole Street.

The last letter she wrote from Torquay makes a slip-of-the-pen error in its date: 31 August 1831. How she must have wished to turn the clock back some ten years! That letter also contains this revealing passage, '. . . the associations of this place lie upon me, struggle as I may, like the oppression of a perpetual nightmare. It is an instinct of self-preservation which impels me to escape—or try to escape.'

Finally, she was allowed to make the journey home to London in an invalid carriage on 1 September 1841. A bed was

[124]

fitted into the conveyance which took her by slow stages to Wimpole Street, arriving there on 11 September. In a letter to Miss Mitford, written from Wimpole Street, she refers to the recent past, 'The scars of that anguish I shall take down with me to the grave.'

In London she resided in a bedroom of the house, dominated by an authoritarian, possessive and unreasonable father. She received few visitors and remained ill but not idle. She wrote critiques and reviews, and she wrote poetry and letters. She had the attentions of a large and caring family but lived a quiet life and seemed destined to continue to do so—until a letter arrived from Robert Browning.

In Wimpole Street, she had composed the two-volume *Poems*, published in 1844. One of the poems of the collection, *Lady Geraldine's Courtship,* contained a compliment to Robert Browning, whose position and popularity as a major poet was not then so well established as her own. Her hero reads to his lady from a variety of poets and refers favourably to the work of the unknown Browning.

Browning returned the compliment in a letter of 10 January 1845, which lacks the conventional salutation but rushes headlong into this effusive opening: 'I love your verses with all my heart, dear Miss Barrett . . .' As if foretelling the future, he continued, 'I do, as I say, love these books with all my heart—and I love you too.'

He was thirty-two and she was thirty-eight when Browning wrote the first of nearly six hundred letters which passed between them. The mutual respect and friendship deepened into love after they met, for the first time, on 20 May 1845.

Under Browning's guidance and encouragement, her health improved rapidly. But the match could never receive the approval of an imperious father who was simply opposed to the marriage of any of his children. The couple were secretly married on 12 September 1845, and they eloped to Italy on the 19th, living happily in Florence, and writing poetry, until she died peacefully in his arms on 29 June 1861.

Elizabeth Barrett Browning was a fortunate woman, able to

overcome grief and ill health by an inner strength and integrity. She enjoyed a happy childhood and had an affectionate, admiring family. She derived great satisfaction from being immersed in the study of language and literature and was able to indulge freely. In middle life, the best was yet to be. An apparently incurable invalid, she met and married the devoted poet, regained her health, had a child, lived in a wonderful city and relished the company of many good friends. Perhaps what is more important, she was a successful and loved human being and poet.

EVELYN WAUGH

at

EASTON COURT HOTEL
CHAGFORD
DEVON

I came to Chagford with the intention of
starting on an ambitious novel tomorrow
morning. I still have a cold and am low in
spirits but I feel full of literary power which
only this evening gives place to qualms of
impotence.

Diary, 31 January 1944

Imagine a small thatched Tudor house of the fifteenth century
set in a lovely garden presided over by a flowering chestnut
tree. Imagine it surrounded by the serene and unspoiled
countryside of Devon. Imagine an interior of enormous
charm and character with log fires, comfortable chairs and
original oak beams. Now imagine that a well-known writer
wanted to escape to the peace and quiet and comfort of a place
conducive to his getting on with his work. Unreal? Perhaps.
But the elements pieced together make up the real story of
Evelyn Waugh at the Easton Court Hotel.

Recommendations are the best way of discovering a good
hotel suitable to one's needs, and the Easton Court Hotel was
recommended to Evelyn by his brother Alec who had discovered it while touring the west country with friends. A
maid became infatuated with their chauffeur, and the
chauffeur persuaded the group to make the hotel their base.
Poetic justice was done when the group became infatuated
with the hotel.

Both brothers, the only children of publisher and literary
critic Arthur Waugh, achieved literary fame. Alec, five years

[127]

older, began to use the hotel as a retreat for his own writing. It was a cosy place with a country house atmosphere run by Mrs Carolyn Cobb, an American, who had a fine appreciation of writers and their needs. And the many writers who came to the hotel had a great respect for her in turn.

The hotel has changed hands since the days of Mrs Cobb but remains essentially unchanged. A sitting room with a great stone fireplace, a bar and a well-stocked library have antique oak furniture and log fires. Eight bedrooms are individually and tastefully furnished. The meals (served in a handsome dining room) feature local game and fish and fresh vegetables mostly grown in the hotel's own garden. Cheese and Devonshire cream come from a local farm.

On entering the village, a signpost declares: 'Chagford, Ancient Stannery Town, 1305'—and the treat begins. In the centre of Chagford is an attractive octagonal Victorian market building which blends in with Tudor and Georgian houses. Older thatched cottages and a sixteenth-century bridge, over the River Teign, make this appealing village on the edge of Dartmoor a delightful centre for exploration. The hotel is situated a mile from the village.

The scenery is glorious, and the possibilities of delightful walks, endless. Stone circles, cromlechs and Bronze Age settlements are there. The River Teign, known for its salmon and trout fishing, winds through the area and is just a few hundred yards from the hotel. By contrast, the great cathedral city of Exeter is just eighteen miles away. Facilities for horse riding, golf, hunting and fishing are plentiful. One might append writing to the list of activities, for the setting has been an inspiration to the creative process of many.

Evelyn Waugh's reputation as a leading novelist was already established when he first came to Chagford. His writing career was launched in 1928 with his first novel, *Decline and Fall*, which was a success. Also in that year came his first marriage which was a failure. He busied himself in the following years by travelling a great deal and writing a great deal. In addition to his travel books and biographies, the

Evelyn Waugh
(1903–1966) used to
retire to the tranquility
of the Easton Court
Hotel, Chagford, to
write

novels of this period include *Vile Bodies* (1930), *Black Mischief* (1932), *A Handful of Dust* (1934) and *Scoop* (1938).

In 1937 he married Laura Herbert and settled into Piers Court in the Gloucestershire Cotswolds for nearly twenty years. Laura pottered about the farm which produced milk, cream, butter and eggs. They travelled, and a trip to Hollywood (where he refused a film offer for *Brideshead Revisited*) resulted in *The Loved One* (1948).

They moved to the west country, to Combe Florey near Taunton, with a large family which by then included six children. Over the final ten-year period at his country home, he declined and fell, and death came on 10 April 1966 at the age of sixty-three.

Although his rate of writing and his energy diminished in his last ten years, he produced four more books. He never stopped writing. Although he put out remarkable quantities of material in his peak period, and claims to have written *Put Out More Flags* while on a troopship returning to England in 1941, Evelyn Waugh seems to have needed a comfortable writing place free from distractions. As early as 1931, he expresses in a letter his intention to go to the Easton Court Hotel: 'Well at Chagford I pretend to my London chums that I am going to hunt stags but to you who are intimates & confidantes I dont mind saying that I shall sit all day in my bedroom writing books, articles, short stories, reviews, plays, cinema scenarios, etc. etc. until I have got a lot more money.'

Apparently he succeeded, for he kept returning to the hotel. He was back in Chagford in April 1932 finishing *Black Mischief*, and he came again and again whenever he needed to get writing done. A letter from the hotel written in 1934 divulges an interesting bit of news, 'I am back & this is my address until the novel is finished . . . The name of the novel is A HANDFUL OF ASHES.' He later changed the title but not the venue.

These entries written in the *Diaries* in October 1939 indicate his work habits at the hotel in Chagford:

Tuesday 24 October: Wrote all morning. The second chapter taking shape and more important ideas springing. A long and lonely walk in the afternoon. A little more work.

Wednesday 25 October: Wrote all the morning and some of the afternoon. Eight-mile walk . . .

Thursday 26 October: Working well. Over 4,000 words done since I arrived . . .

Friday 27 October: Working well . . .

But it was not all work and no play. He did take exhilarating walks, and Laura often came down to meet him and sometimes to spend the day with him in Exeter. On Sundays he generally attended church services in the tiny village of Gidleigh. And there was the occasional happy telephone interruption, once with a message to announce that Laura had had a baby.

However, it was not always perfection at the hotel, as this *Diary* excerpt of February 1944 suggests. 'The hotel is full of elderly women who do not distract me from my work. Carolyn has given me the room they call "the middle lounge" for a private sitting room but the fire smokes so badly that I must choose between freezing and going blind.'

When he was ready to begin his 'ambitious novel,' *Brideshead Revisited*, Evelyn Waugh revisited this simple country place which is a far cry from the half-legendary stately home of England that he calls Brideshead. Again, a few extracts from the *Diaries* of 1944 record the successful piling up of words at Easton Court:

Wednesday 2 February: Score at close of play 3,000 words odd.

Tuesday 8 February: Working steadily . . .

Sunday 13 February: . . . rewriting . . .

Monday 14 February: 3,000 words in three hours. I shall have the third chapter done before I go to bed.

Friday 18 February–Wednesday 23 February: Laura came to stay with me . . .

Saturday 26 February: This morning I finished my third chapter, 33,000 words in all, and took it in high good humour to the post office . . .

A footnote to the completed manuscript of *Brideshead Revisited* reads, 'Chagford (Devon), Feb–June 1944.'

To say that the Easton Court Hotel played a great role in the life of Evelyn Waugh would be to understate the truth. More accurately, it was part author of the novels. It presents a record of work well done in a congenial atmosphere. Other artists would agree, for the guest book is signed by such illustrious names as John Betjeman, John Gielgud, Dr Margaret Meade, Ralph Richardson, C. P. Snow and John Steinbeck.

The temptation is to think that one need only repair to the Easton Court Hotel for the words to pile up. While the proprietors do not guarantee that their guests will produce novels of distinction, they do promise a charming Tudor house in a gorgeous country spot which serves as an excellent centre from which to explore Dartmoor or Devon. And at the very least, the guest may write a postcard or two telling of a memorable holiday experience.

GEORGE BERNARD SHAW

at

THE VICTORIA HOTEL
SIDMOUTH
DEVON

Well, what more could anyone ask but a nice
hotel? All the housekeeping done for us: no
trouble with the servants: no rates nor taxes. I
have never had any peace except in a hotel . . .

The Millionairess

George Bernard Shaw was eighty-two when he first came to
the Victoria Hotel in Sidmouth in 1938. His wife and friends
cajoled and conspired to get him to go at a time when he was
feeling worn out and unwell. And no wonder! So prolific, so
active and creative was he throughout his life, that it is
meaningless to say that he is famous or popular or talented.
He wrote five novels, about fifty plays, innumerable pieces of
journalism and vast amounts of drama and music criticism.
He was a lecturer and a member of the Fabian Society.

Born in Dublin on 26 July 1856, he left for London in 1876
determined to become a successful writer. He had a long
apprenticeship, and fame eluded him until he was fifty. When
it came his success was stupendous, culminating in the
Nobel Prize for Literature awarded in 1926 when he was
seventy.

His first play, *Widowers' Houses*, was performed in 1892.
Then came *The Philanderer, Mrs Warren's Profession*, and
Arms and the Man. His fifth play, *Candida*, ushered in a long
line of plays with hardly a pause—*The Man of Destiny, You
Never Can Tell, The Devil's Disciple, Caesar and Cleopatra* . . .

The important man of the theatre became involved with
several attractive and important ladies of the theatre. Always

[133]

in search of leading ladies for his plays, his attempts to win them over knew no bounds. He often fell in love with them. Fascinated by the acting of Ellen Terry, he wrote letters to her as early as 1892, and he later wrote *Captain Brassbound's Conversion* for her. During his years as a drama critic for the *Saturday Review*, he came to admire Mrs Patrick Campbell for her beauty and for her talent as an actress. In August 1912, he began a correspondence of love letters with her—Stella— and of course he wrote plays for her.

Shaw was busy with his correspondence with Ellen Terry when he met Charlotte Frances Payne-Townshend. She became his secretary by the beginning of 1898 and his wife in June of that year. Seen by many as a nurse and mother to him, they got along splendidly together, sharing interests and a long life. The couple lived in such places as Haslemere and Hindhead before settling in 1906 into 'Shaw's Corner' in Ayot St Lawrence, a pretty, little, isolated village in Hertfordshire of the kind one is in danger of missing by blinking an eye. Shaw disliked the house but stayed on rather than undertake the bothersome alternative of leaving it.

Shaw's Corner is an unpretentious but delightful house now run by the National Trust and open to visitors who make their way to it via difficult single-track country lanes. The four downstairs rooms and their contents remain as they were in Shaw's lifetime with such personal treasures and effects on display as his pens, typewriter and desk. His hats hang on a rack in the entrance hall as if in readiness to be picked up by him on his way out for a long walk or a long bicycle ride. In the garden is the summerhouse retreat in which he did his writing. At Shaw's Corner, Shaw could relax as well as work.

Charlotte was not musical, nor was she greatly interested in theatre. And she abhorred the hero-worshippers who fawned, no matter where they went, on the author of *Man and Superman, Major Barbara, Misalliance, Pygmalion, Heartbreak House, Saint Joan, The Millionairess*. But it was a long and successful marriage and one based on her condition that the marriage should not be consummated.

[134]

George Bernard
Shaw (1856–1950)
used the
fire-escape to avoid
appearing publicly
at The Victoria
Hotel, Sidmouth

Other eccentricities might include the fact that Shaw was a vegetarian and a teetotaller with a strong aversion to tobacco. His idea of a holiday was a change in work, and he did not indulge in travel. Charlotte, on the other hand, had a passion for travel. Perhaps it was her total distaste for housekeeping that made her prefer hotel life. Nevertheless, Shaw agreed to go to Sidmouth.

The nature of his illness was unknown. He had been overworking in 1937, as usual, and was feeling tired and irritable; Charlotte became concerned and enlisted the aid of friends. Nora and St John Ervine investigated several hotels before selecting the Victoria Hotel in Sidmouth as the one that would meet their requirements. Their comfortable suite at the hotel consisted of two bedrooms and a sitting room. The manager was so helpful and solicitous that they returned to his care at a later date.

At the Victoria, Shaw resented being gaped at by guests who recognised his gaunt figure, and he developed the habit of using the fire-escape to enter or leave his sitting room, thereby upsetting several elderly ladies.

In order to distract Shaw from his illness, various jaunts were made. One excursion took them to Ashe House in nearby Musbury, the house in which the Duke of Marlborough was born. But Shaw displayed more interest in the archery range than in the house. He also exhibited a complete indifference to nature. They drove through a beautiful valley, thick and blue with flowers. 'Did you see the bluebells, GBS?' asked Charlotte. He replied, 'What bluebells?' Indeed, his works contain few references to the beauties of nature.

He had arrived in Sidmouth at the end of April 1938, and during the several weeks spent at the Victoria his health seemed to improve. But by May his condition deteriorated, and Charlotte insisted on a doctor. The diagnosis was pernicious anaemia, and he had to undergo a course of liver injections in opposition to his vegetarian principles. He was in his eighties, but he rallied and was quite well by October.

Charlotte died in 1943, aged eighty-six. Shaw continued to

write, largely political works. His last completed play, *Buoyant Billions*, was written in 1946 at the age of ninety. In 1949 he wrote *Farfetched Fables* and *Sixteen Self Sketches*.

One day, at the age of ninety-four, he went into his garden to prune trees and had the accident which ended his life. He stepped back from a tree, slipped, fell and broke his leg. At home after being treated in hospital, he did not recover. Death came on 2 November 1950.

The wit and humour of his works make it a pleasure to recall George Bernard Shaw. It is a particular pleasure to remember him at Sidmouth, an attractive seaside resort with Regency and early Victorian architecture. Sidmouth was once a popular watering place and retreat for the aristocracy. Queen Victoria made her first visit to it as an infant, in 1819.

From the hotel, the town centre is within easy walking distance, and surrounding the town is a wealth and a variety of natural beauty. Walking is a good pastime, especially along the cliff-top paths which overlook the beaches and coastline.

The fine Edwardian hotel has been offering high standards of comfort and service since it opened its doors to guests in 1904. Sixty-two bedrooms are individually designed and all are comfortable. Many have balconies and most have views of the sea. A light and airy sun lounge with views across the gardens to Sidmouth Bay, cheerful bars, a writing room—all the public rooms offer relaxation.

Well-maintained and refurbished since Shaw's visit, the hotel has every amenity available: indoor and outdoor swimming pools, sauna, solarium, billiard room, tennis court and eighteen-hole putting green.

Let us allow a character in Shaw's *The Millionairess* (written only two years before Shaw came to the Victoria Hotel) have the final words: 'This is what home ought to be, though it's only a hotel.'

CHARLES KINGSLEY

at

THE ROYAL HOTEL
BIDEFORD
NORTH DEVON

All who have travelled through the delicious
scenery of North Devon must needs know the
little white town of Bideford, which slopes
upwards from its broad tide-river paved with
yellow sands, and many-arched old bridge
where salmon wait for Autumn floods, toward
the pleasant upland on the west.

Westward Ho!

There is no seaside town in Dorset called French
Lieutenant's Woman—or even Persuasion. But there *is* a
seaside town in Devon called Westward Ho!

An obscure place until it was given the name of Charles
Kingsley's popular novel, Westward Ho! is a resort town
consisting mostly of holiday homes, amusement or leisure
centres, good bathing beaches and a golf course. Located on
the northern Devonshire coast, it is in effect an extension of
Bideford, the town in which Charles Kingsley lived in 1854
when he wrote *Westward Ho!*

Born on 12 June 1819 at the parsonage in Holne, one of the
most attractive villages of Devonshire, Charles Kingsley
learned to love the sea, the country and the outdoor life. As a
child, he was moved about from place to place whenever his
father, a vicar, received a new appointment. Barnack in the
Fens District of Lincolnshire and the lovely picture-book
Devon village of Clovelly were later to appear in his writing.
The mystery and charm of the fenlands is described in his
final novel of 1866, *Hereward the Wake,* and Clovelly
appeared disguised as Aberalva in *Two Years Ago.*

[138]

Charles Kingsley (1819–1875) wrote his novel *Westward Ho!* in an upstairs study of a rented house in Bideford, now part of The Royal Hotel

When he was seventeen, the family emigrated to London. Charles deeply regretted the loss of open country and returned to his native Devon whenever he could. He entered King's College, London and afterwards, Magdalene College, Cambridge. Ordained as an Anglican clergyman at the age of twenty-three, he was appointed rector at Eversley in Hampshire. Together with his loving wife Fanny, whom he married early in 1844, he was to make Eversley his permanent home for the next thirty-three years—until his death on 23 January 1876.

From his childhood, Charles Kingsley had written poetry. His principal poetic works are *The Saint's Tragedy* (1848), a drama of Elizabeth of Hungary as she is torn between her natural desires and her religious duties, and *Andromeda* (1858), which deals with classical myth. But it was as a novelist that he made his literary mark.

A man of action with a deep concern about social conditions of England, Charles Kingsley put his ideas into fictional form. *Yeast* was originally written in instalments for *Fraser's Magazine* and published in book form in 1851. In *Alton Locke* (1850), he continued his fight to improve conditions for the poor working classes. His novels had the purpose of instructing, arousing public opinion and changing conditions but his main fault is that he preaches. He gave sermons from his pulpit and he gave sermons in his novels, and although *Hypatia* (1853) was an historical novel set in fifth-century Alexandria, it too included topics of current concern and aroused wide public interest.

Winters were hard in Eversley, and the damp and cold Eversley rectory aggravated Fanny's precarious state of health. In July 1854, the Kingsley family moved temporarily to a house in Bideford in the hope that the change of climate would be beneficial to her. Furthermore, Charles Kingsley wanted to be near the scene of the novel he was writing. Bideford was a total success. Mrs Kingsley's health improved, and *Westward Ho!* was published early in 1855.

Bideford was the principal port of north Devon from the

time Sir Richard Grenville secured a charter from Queen Elizabeth. Kingsley extracted the local colour of Bideford for his adventure story set in an earlier age: 'Pleasantly the old town stands there . . . fanned day and night by the fresh ocean breeze, which forbids alike the keen winter frosts, and the fierce thunder heats of the midland; and pleasantly it has stood there for now, perhaps, eight hundred years . . .'

He used scenes of the surrounding countryside and coast which he knew and loved to present vivid pictures of Elizabethan heroes who appear in the pages of his novel—Drake, Raleigh, Frobisher. His accurate historical account and excellent descriptive power made the book immensely successful. Although he needed to confine the setting of his stories to places familiar to him, it is curious that he also did a superb job of painting the scenery of the West Indies, which he was not to know until he visited some fourteen years later.

Curiously too, *Westward Ho!* has survived primarily as an adventure story for boys, full of sword fights and galloping horses, rather than as a polemical Protestant tract and perhaps his most violently propagandist novel. His prejudiced viewpoint did not allow him to be fair to Catholicism. It dwells on Spanish atrocities and glosses over English ones. The bloodthirsty massacres are extreme, and he himself called it a 'sanguinary' book.

Kingsley wanted to inspire young Englishmen to be as heroic as the models of the past. Many regarded it not only as a stirring adventure story but as recruiting propaganda at a time when England was engaged in the Crimean War. But the public approved of his views and the book met with popular and critical success, making him a leading novelist of the day.

Kingsley worked on *Westward Ho!* in an upstairs study of his rented Bideford house. Built by a wealthy merchant in 1688, the house has since been incorporated into what is now the Royal Hotel.

The Royal Hotel stands on a busy corner of the town, overlooking the River Torridge and the 'many-arched old bridge'. With its twenty-four arches, the Bideford Bridge is the town's most prominent sight. Here are two reminders that nothing is wasted in England: the bridge, which was widened in 1925, incorporates part of the ancient bridge of 1460; and the Royal Hotel, which opened in 1888, encompasses the original house of 1688 in which Kingsley wrote.

The hotel retains the large oak-panelled room with a magnificent moulded plaster ceiling, appropriately named the Kingsley Room, for in it the author worked hard on his famous novel. Across the corridor is the Kingsley Bedroom with marble fireplace surround and plasterwork ceiling, nicely furnished to evoke a feeling of the author's presence. The grand oak staircase leading to these rooms is another original part of the merchant's mansion.

Many other features give the hotel the interest and charm of age. The covered courtyard of the hotel was formerly the stable yard of the old mansion and is now the ballroom, while the present dining room occupies the site of the stables. Part of the old building was once used as a workhouse and later as a prison. Three cells remain with heavy double-planked doors and sliding peep holes.

It is an old-fashioned hotel in an old-fashioned town. Though a bit tired, the town has character: several seventeenth-century buildings of architectural interest can be seen in Bridgeland Road and a Pannier Market is held on Tuesdays and Saturdays.

No escape is possible from reminders of the author's presence. Alongside the river and near the end of the quay the inevitable statue stands, predictably in Kingsley Road. All about are tributes to his name—Kingsley Plumbing, Kingsley Car Sales, Kingsley Pet Stores, Kingsley Dry Cleaners, Kingsley Insurance . . .

After *Westward Ho!* Kingsley wrote *Two Years Ago*, a novel which takes place in 1854 and deals with a cholera epidemic and a young doctor who attempts to halt it by improving sanitation. The author had actually campaigned for better sanitary conditions to prevent cholera outbreaks.

Kingsley is also remembered for *The Water Babies*, a children's story of a chimney sweep who escapes a tyrannical master to live in a watery world. Like many other complex and lasting children's stories, this minor masterpiece can take on added levels of meaning to give satisfaction to adult readers.

Many of his other works cover history and sermons which are remarkable for style, diversity of subject and humanity. *At Last* (1871) records the realisation of a travel dream which was at last fulfilled when he visited the West Indies—his mother's home—in 1869.

Although Kingsley was also known as a social reformer, sanitary reformer, editor, critic and reviewer, naturalist and populariser of geology and zoology, although he became Canon of Chester and of Westminster, Chaplain to the Queen, and Professor of History at Cambridge, he achieved prominence primarily as an author of novels and particularly as the author of *Westward Ho!* To him we owe the existence of perhaps the only town in the world with an exclamation mark in its name!

at

ALFOXTON PARK HOTEL
HOLFORD
SOMERSET

> But never elsewhere in one place I knew
> So many nightingales.
>> *The Nightingale*
>> Samuel Taylor Coleridge

> It is the first mild day of March.
> Each minute, sweeter than before,
> The redbreast sings from the tall larch
> That stands beside our door.
>> *To My Sister*
>> William Wordsworth

> A very bright moonlight night. Venus
> like another moon. Lost to us at
> Alfoxden long before she goes down the
> large white sea.
>> *The Alfoxden Journal*
>> Dorothy Wordsworth

Although associated primarily with the Lake District, Wordsworth—together with his close friend Coleridge—can be said to have started poetic life in Somerset, in the west country rather than in the lakes.

In 1795 Wordsworth and Coleridge met at Bristol, and the meeting was to bring about a literary revolution. Samuel Taylor Coleridge moved, in 1796, with his wife and infant son to Nether Stowey in Somerset, to a small cottage in Lime Street now maintained by the National Trust. Before long, William Wordsworth moved with his sister Dorothy from Racedown in Dorset to Holford in Somerset to be near

Before William Wordsworth (1770–1850) ever
went to the Lake District he lived in Somerset,
with his sister Dorothy, at Alfoxton House,
where Coleridge (1772–1834) stayed with them.
It is now The Alfoxton Park Hotel.

Coleridge. Wordsworth was in a state of severe depression and despair brought on by lost ideals pertaining to the French Revolution and by guilt incurred by the need to leave Annette Vallon and their child behind in France.

William and Dorothy rented Alfoxden House, half a mile west of the village of Holford, just a few miles from Nether Stowey. They installed themselves in the early eighteenth-century manor house of the St Albyn family in July 1797, and Coleridge stayed with them during their first week at Alfoxden. Thus began an idyllic year in which the three were virtually inseparable.

Dorothy loved the spacious and elegant house and called it 'that dear and beautiful place'. William wrote of its 'enchanting beauty'. Their Alfoxden home (as spelled by Dorothy in her *Journal* but pronounced Allfoxen by the locals) is now the Alfoxton Park Hotel.

The present gracious white house, with roof of bluish slate, is set in grounds which consist of fifty acres of gardens and deer park; the grounds also include an outdoor heated swimming pool and tennis court. The front door opened onto a grass court and gravel path on which Wordsworth paced when he was creating poetry. Gone is the larch, with its resident redbreast, that stood near the door.

The comfortable, family-run hotel faces the Quantock hills and commands a wonderful view of the Bristol Channel with Wales on the far side. From their dining room, the Wordsworths could feast on a pastoral landscape which took in the view of the sea. Walkers still encounter sheep grazing on the slopes; their owners are still given rights of free pasture.

The walled kitchen garden which Dorothy once tended, and which produced lettuces and other basic provisions for the meals she prepared, now supplies some of the ingredients which go into the chef's good meals, served in the Georgian Dining Room.

The mansion, as Dorothy called it, had nine bedrooms but after the Wordsworths left an extension was added on the north side. Today the hotel has twenty bedrooms, including a four-poster room. Most bedrooms have adjoining private bathrooms.

The Oak Room Bar was Wordsworth's library. In the long panelled parlour to the right of the entrance, Coleridge gave his first reading of *The Ancient Mariner* by the warmth of a fireplace decorated with blue and white Dutch tiles picturing windmills and ships.

The Wordsworths paid £23 rent for the idyllic year, a sum that would today only partially cover a single idyllic day. Dorothy wrote of the area in a letter: 'There is everything here; sea, woods wild as fancy ever painted, brooks clear and pebbly as in Cumberland, villages so romantic; and William and I, in a wander by ourselves, found out a sequestered waterfall in a dell formed by steep hills covered with full-grown timber trees.' There was everything there. Primarily, there was Coleridge. 'We are three people, but only one soul,' said Coleridge. They were together almost daily: they walked, read, discussed poetry, enjoyed sunshine, gazed at views, exchanged ideas and thoughts.

The friends were continually wandering over the Quan-tocks, and the contemporary wanderer can seek inspiration by following their footsteps, perhaps with Dorothy's *Alfoxden Journal* as guide: 'On the hill-tops . . . through the wood to Holford . . . followed the sheep tracks . . . to Stowey . . . to Woodlands, and to the waterfall . . . into the Coombe . . . walked . . . walked by moonlight . . . walked to the sea-side . . . walked to Cheddar . . .'

Coleridge and Wordsworth collaborated on the *Lyrical Ballads*, which inaugurates the Romantic movement in English literature. Almost all of the poems of that volume were written in the spring and summer of 1798.

At Alfoxden, Coleridge had listened to 'delicious notes' and wrote *The Nightingale* for the *Lyrical Ballads*. Confined to his cottage when his wife accidentally spilled a pan of scalding milk over his foot, Coleridge imagined in 'This Lime-Tree Bower, My Prison' the wanderings of Dorothy and William over hilltops with their visitor, Charles Lamb.

Coleridge's *Rime of the Ancient Mariner* is a reminder that the sea was only about two miles away; one of their walks took in the ancient little port of Watchet, the supposed prototype of the ancient mariner's harbour. *Christabel* and *Kubla Khan* are among the greatest of his poems, all of which were written during this happy period.

Wordsworth expressed his joy in nature, which outweighs the evils in man, in *Lines Written in Early Spring*. And in the spring he composed the companion pieces, *Expostulation and Reply* and *The Tables Turned*, in front of the house at Alfoxden.

Nor can Dorothy's influence on both poets be overestimated. For Coleridge, Dorothy was 'exquisite in mind and heart'. For Wordsworth, she was a source of ideas. Consider, for example, this extract from her *Journal:* '25 January 1798— Went to Poole's after tea. The sky spread over with one continuous cloud, whitened by the light of the moon, which, though her dim shape was seen, did not throw forth so strong a light as to chequer the earth with shadows. At once the clouds seemed to cleave asunder, and left her in the centre of a black-blue vault.'

Wordsworth adopted the imagery for his poem, *A Night-piece:*

The sky is overcast
With a continuous cloud of texture close,
Heavy and wan, all whitened by the Moon,
Which through that veil is indistinctly seen,
A dull, contracted circle, yielding light
So feebly spread that not a shadow falls,
Chequering the ground—from rock, plant, tree, or tower.
At length a pleasant instantaneous gleam
Startles the pensive traveller while he treads
His lonesome path, with unobserving eye
Bent earthwards; he looks up—the clouds are split
Asunder,—and above his head he sees
The clear Moon, and the glory of the heavens.

[148]

There in a black-blue vault she sails along,
Followed by multitudes of stars . . .

When their one-year lease expired in July 1798, the Wordsworths were refused a renewal and forced to leave because of their questionable activities. They had done so much walking, including nocturnal rambles, that they were suspected of being spies at a time when everyone feared invasion by the French. Even Coleridge expressed his forebodings and anxieties in *Fears in Solitude* in April of that year.

But the year had worked its wonders. Coleridge reached the peak of his creative power during this, the happiest year of his life. Dorothy too had enjoyed her least troubled time, a year full of the contentment and health that later years would lack. And Wordsworth left cured of depression, with self-confidence and happiness restored, and with his destiny as a poet ensured.

What became of the threesome? In a state of poor health, Coleridge had been taking opium for relief of pain and suffered the effects of addiction. At the age of forty-three, he put himself into the hands and home of a London physician for the remaining years of his life, continuing to produce important work. When he died in 1834, Wordsworth mourned him as the 'most *wonderful* man' he had ever known.

Born in 1770 at Cockermouth in the Lake District, Wordsworth returned with Dorothy to the Lakes in 1799 to settle there finally.

Curiously enough, both Coleridge and Wordsworth returned to Alfoxden. Coleridge visited his friend Tom Poole in Nether Stowey around 1807 for the last time. The visit that was to last two weeks took two months. He and Poole rode together over the Quantocks and around Alfoxden, recalling those old walks and blissful months with Dorothy and William.

Wordsworth returned forty-three years later to visit his youthful haunts. In 1841, he had gone with his wife, Mary

Hutchinson, to Bath where he stayed with their good friend
Miss Isabella Fenwick in a house in North Parade, now the
Grosvenor Steak House. (A tablet on the front of the building
bears the inscription: 'Here dwelt William Wordsworth.')
The Wordsworths drove from Bath to Ashcott to have breakfast at Piper's Inn with their newly-married daughter Dora
and her husband. Afterwards they all went to Alfoxden where
he sought nostalgic reminiscences of the past.

Who knows what poetry or great thoughts may inspire
today's visitor to the lovely Alfoxton Park Hotel? The
influence on Wordsworth was ever present. In the last book of
the *Prelude* written in 1850, the year of his death, he refers to
that crucial and idyllic summer with Coleridge:

> . . . but, beloved Friend!
> When, looking back, thou seest, in clearer view
> Than any liveliest sight of yesterday,
> That summer, under whose indulgent skies,
> Upon smooth Quantock's airy ridge we roved
> Unchecked, or loitered 'mid her sylvan combs,
> Thou in bewitching words, with happy heart,
> Didst chaunt the vision of that Ancient Man,
> The bright-eyed Mariner, and rueful woes
> Didst utter of the Lady Christabel.

BENJAMIN DISRAELI

at

THE ROYAL BATH HOTEL
BOURNEMOUTH
DORSET

I am going to Bournemouth—the Bath
Hotel—some rooms on the first floor, I hope
pretty good as Rothschilds have them now.

Letter to Lady Bradford,
23 November 1874

Benjamin Disraeli was an author long before he was a
politician. He produced his first novel when he was in his
early twenties, and he went on writing throughout his life.
From *Vivian Grey*, in 1826, when he was twenty-two, to
Endymion in 1880, the year before he died, he had a long,
prolific and diverse literary career. In addition to his eleven
novels, he wrote short stories, poems, a biography, a play and
essays.

The only Prime Minister ever to write novels, Disraeli is
generally accepted today as a skilful and accomplished writer
whose neglected works deserve a better fate. Perhaps his
powerful political career obscured the merits of his literary
output. The noted critic F. R. Leavis says that he deserves to
be revived as a novelist and that his so-called 'Young England'
trilogy expresses 'the interests of a supremely intelligent
politician who has a sociologist's understanding of civilisation and its movement in his time'.

His oeuvre is generally divided into three groups—those
books written in his pre-Parliamentary days, the trilogy
written in the midst of his political career, and the last two
novels produced after he became Prime Minister.

[151]

The first phase begins with *Vivian Grey* which features a clever and ambitious hero whose schemes are defeated. It was followed in 1831 by Disraeli's rendition of fashionable life, *The Young Duke*, which he himself described as half fashion and half passion. A sixteen-month tour of the Near East gave him the atmosphere for *Contarini Fleming* in 1832 and *Alroy* in 1833. He wrote both *Henrietta Temple* (a novel of love and manners) and *Venetia* (a fictional account of the lives of Byron and Shelley) in 1837 to relieve financial pressure. It was also the year in which he won a seat in Parliament and shortly thereafter, in 1839, he married Mary Anne Lewis, a widow.

The trio of novels of the 1840s belonging to the second group are considered by most critics to be the most significant: *Coningsby* (1844), *Sybil* (1845) and *Tancred* (1847).

Coningsby encompasses the period from the passing of the Reform Bill in 1832 to the Tory victory in 1841 and ends with Harry Coningsby's election to Parliament. In *Sybil, or The Two Nations*, the two nations of the alternate title are identified as the rich and the poor, and Disraeli exposes the oppressive tyranny of an industrial system which causes human misery. The eponymous hero of *Tancred* is a young, religious enthusiast who goes to the Holy Land in search of revelation and truth, and the central theme is the discovery of religious faith.

Taken together, the trilogy expressed the ideals of a group of bright, young and dynamic Parliamentarians who made up the 'Young England' movement. Greatly concerned with the well-being of man, they called for past ideals to be applied to present Tory party principles and they chose Disraeli to describe their aims. This he did in the trilogy, thereby extending his political ideology into the realm of imaginative writing. The novels deal with the social problems of the time. They give the daily workings of politics and embody Disraeli's own experiences of political intrigue.

After a long interval of twenty-three years, Disraeli returned to the novel in 1870 with *Lothair*, followed in 1880

Benjamin
Disraeli
(1804–1881)
nursed his gout at
The Royal Bath
Hotel,
Bournemouth

by *Endymion*. He wrote the final novel when he was seventy-seven and out of office, and he was hard at work on another at the time of his death.

With his vivid accounts of English political life, his acute observations and his talent for narrative and witty dialogue, his works are good enough to be remembered in literary annals even if he had never been a statesman. But he did become a powerful statesman—leader of the Tory party and Prime Minister of England.

Disraeli was first elected to Parliament in 1837 after five unsuccessful attempts. The long hiatus that occurred in his writing career would seem to be due to total absorption in his life as a statesman. In 1852 he became Chancellor of the Exchequer for just a few months and again in 1858 and in 1866. Two years later he became Prime Minister, for a short term of eleven months, and then leader of the opposition for six years. It was during his second term of office as Prime Minister, from 1874 to 1880, that he stayed at the Royal Bath Hotel in Bournemouth.

Disraeli suffered from a case of acute gout throughout 1874, which was first diagnosed in that February. He had several attacks and was often too ill to be present at Parliamentary sessions. Because of his poor physical condition, Queen Victoria recommended 'the very salubrious air of Bournemouth'. She had not herself been there, but Sir James Clark, her physician and a resident of Bournemouth, believed in the efficacy of the sea air to produce a cure. Disraeli stayed at the hotel from November 1874 to January 1875 and although he was extremely unwell when he arrived, he was able to report to the Queen on his return for the January cabinet meetings that his health was greatly improved.

But Disraeli had to be cajoled and persuaded to go to Bournemouth. A letter to Lady Bradford written on 18 November 1874 expresses his dislike of hotels in general: 'There is a great discomfort for a person like me in an hotel life—forced to order and eat dinners and drink wines and live in rooms like barracks, and no comforts and accommodations.

It is horrid . . .' He was predisposed to complain, and complain he did—about the food (frightful), the weather (savage climate) and the resort itself (a large overgrown watering place). He missed the comforts of his Hughenden home, with his books and beeches, and later expressed regret at not having gone instead to Hughenden, the country estate in Buckinghamshire to which he had moved in 1848. Nevertheless he expressed to Queen Victoria, from Bournemouth on 10 December 1874, the certainty that '. . . the visit to this place, which your Majesty yourself deigned to recommend, will turn out a great success.'

Bournemouth was promoted by physicians for its healthy sea air and good climate, but weather conditions were harsh that season. Disraeli writes in a Christmas Eve letter to Lady Bradford: 'The severe weather has been very trying to me; but I hope it has not materially thrown me back and now the frost has vanished.'

There are further complaints, in a letter of December 1874 to Lady Chesterfield, about having to remain indoors due to adverse weather conditions: 'Everything is white, the crust on the earth thick and hard and an Easterly wind always.'

He improved in the new year with the change to milder weather and wrote to Lady Chesterfield on 3 January 1875 that 'the thaw has quite revived me and removed all my *malaise.*' He added, no doubt with relief, that he expected to be in London around the 9th.

It was while he was in Bournemouth that Disraeli wrote advising the Queen to confer the highest distinction for literary eminence: a GCB—the Grand Cross of the Order of the Bath—and a pension on Carlyle, and a baronetcy on Tennyson.

He seems to have written no fiction at the Royal Bath Hotel, but he wrote many letters which he posted from a box, now displayed at the Russell-Cotes Museum, very near the hotel. When Bournemouth's first letter box, red with the initials *VR*, stood at the corner of Bath Road it was, we are informed, used by the eminent political opponents Disraeli and

Gladstone. Gladstone, too, came to this Victorian resort for the well-to-do, and he also stayed at the Royal Bath.

From the time the Bath Hotel opened on Queen Victoria's Coronation Day, 28 June 1838, it has sheltered a long list of distinguished guests—Prince Oscar of Sweden, Paderewski, Sir Henry Irving and his leading lady Miss Ellen Terry, Empress Eugenie, and Oscar Wilde. But it only became 'Royal' when royalty visited on 23 September 1856, in the form of the Prince of Wales, later King Edward VII.

The building was acquired in 1876 by Mr Merton Russell-Cotes, who had it redecorated, reconstructed and enlarged. Mr Russell-Cotes became Mayor of Bournemouth in 1894; he opened the first public library in the town and founded the Russell-Cotes Art Gallery and Museum before being knighted in 1911. After he died in 1921, the hotel remained in family control until it was taken over by DeVere Enterprises in 1963.

For a royal treat, the de luxe five-star Royal Bath Hotel is still the place to go. Set in its own gardens overlooking the bay, the hotel is ideally situated. It makes a good centre for seeing such places of interest as Stonehenge, Beaulieu, Salisbury, Longleat and Corfe Castle, or for visiting the town itself, the Sandbourne of Thomas Hardy's Wessex.

In addition to 135 luxury bedrooms, the hotel offers a variety of facilities from indoor gymnasium and sauna to outdoor heated swimming pool. There is an Oak Room for small conferences and the DeVere Suite for larger ones. Disraeli's negative comments notwithstanding, a fine restaurant offers superb dishes in a sumptuous setting. For relaxation, there is the commodious and comfortable main lounge with classical columns and fine plaster ceiling. The Buccaneer Bar is more contemporary. A plunge into the Victorian past is offered in the handsome Disraeli's Bar, warmly decorated in red and enhanced with pictures and a name to honour the very distinguished guest.

On the way out to the Royal Bath Hotel from London, the visitor could perhaps arrange to stop at Hughenden Manor near High Wycombe in Buckinghamshire. The late eighteenth-century white building in which Disraeli lived the life of a country gentleman is most attractive and is maintained for the public by the National Trust.

For a memorable holiday and a continuation of that style of graceful living which Disraeli loved—not necessarily by royal command and preferably without gout—stay awhile at Bournemouth's Royal Bath Hotel.

WALES

LEWIS CARROLL

──────── ★ ★ ★ ────────

at

THE GOGARTH ABBEY HOTEL
WEST SHORE
LLANDUDNO
GWYNEDD
WALES

'A knot!' said Alice, already to make herself
useful, and looking anxiously about her. 'Oh,
do let me help to undo it!'

Alice's Adventures in Wonderland

Perhaps the most significant picnic in literary history took place on 4 July 1862. On that date, the Reverend Charles Lutwidge Dodgson, a young mathematics lecturer at Christ Church, Oxford, embarked on a river excursion. With him went his friend Robinson Duckworth of Trinity College and the three daughters of Dean Liddell of Christ Church: Lorina, aged thirteen; Alice, ten; and Edith, eight.

From Folly Bridge, the party set off on their journey up the Isis to Godstow. As they went along, Dodgson told the story of Alice's adventures. 'Dodgson, is this an extempore romance of yours?' Duckworth asked. The reply was, 'Yes, I'm inventing as we go along.' Three miles up the river the group disembarked to enjoy tea on the bank at a pretty site with the romantic ruins of Godstow Nunnery nearby and the Oxford skyline in the distance. The historic picnic ended with a dessert that the world has been enjoying ever since, for the heroine fell into a rabbit hole, and the author fell into a whole new literary world in which he was to become better known as Lewis Carroll.

[158]

Lewis Carroll (1832–1898). Did he or didn't he visit Alice's family at their holiday home in Llandudno? Now the Gogarth Abbey Hotel.

Back at the Deanery, Alice requested, 'Oh, Mr Dodgson, I wish you would write out Alice's adventures for me.' To oblige the young lady, he sat up nearly all night. Duckworth, the 'Duck' of the story, later persuaded him to publish it, and exactly three years after the famous river expedition, the book with the name *Alice's Adventures Under Ground* appeared.

The beautiful and intelligent Alice Liddell remained his ideal child friend always. They had first met in 1856, just before her fourth birthday. He was twenty-four, an Oxford don, and a shy, stammering bachelor who was also interested in photography. Alice's father was Henry George Liddell, Dean of Christ Church. The Deanery in which the Liddell family lived faced Tom Quad, where Dodgson was one day busily taking photographs of the Christ Church Cathedral. The Liddell children, intrigued by his occupation, engaged him in conversation. A friendship developed. He saw the children constantly, and he photographed them often.

Apparently, he also visited the Liddell family at their holiday house in the Welsh resort town of Llandudno. Then called Pen Morfa, that summer home is now the Gogarth Abbey Hotel. The Welsh resort town of Llandudno has retained its charm despite growing size and popularity. The town proudly persists in its Lewis Carroll connections with a statue of the White Rabbit at the end of the Model Yacht Pond, by a street named Carroll Place, and with a marble font, a gift of school children to the memory of Lewis Carroll, in the Church of Our Saviour.

The main beach, North Shore, with a magnificent crescent bay, is enclosed by two headlands—Great Ormes Head and Little Ormes Head. (Did wild rabbits scurrying over Great Ormes Head suggest the rabbit-hole with which Alice's adventures begin?) The Gogarth Abbey Hotel is located on the West Shore, which has fine views of Conway Bay and a statue of Lewis Carroll. (Did the long stretch of sand provide a setting for the Gryphon and the Mock Turtle?) With forty-one modern bedrooms, a dining room with views across the sea and Lewis Carroll associations, the hotel is an attractive literary shrine.

So far the story is a good one with a great deal of charm, but alas, Dodgson's stay in Llandudno may be as much of a fairy tale as his story of Alice. Lewis Carroll scholars cannot agree, or verify with absolute certainty, that he went to Pen Morfa or indeed whether he ever went to Llandudno at all. What the reader chooses to believe depends to a very large extent on which authority he chooses to read. Such respected sources as *The Oxford Literary Guide to the British Isles* select words carefully: 'C. L. Dodgson is believed to have visited Dean Liddell . . . at his summer residence, Pen Morfa, on the West Shore, now part of the Gogarth Abbey Hotel.' Tourist guides, with the obvious desire to support local tradition, select words less carefully. One points to 'the fact that the author of *Alice in Wonderland* stayed in the town with the Liddells.' What are the facts and/or discrepancies?

First of all, it seems reasonably clear that Dodgson was not on good terms with Alice's parents, who simply did not like him. The formidable Mrs Liddell could be quite abrupt with him, or even rude; so it is not likely that he would have been invited to share their holiday.

If he had stayed at Pen Morfa, surely he would have deemed the event significant enough to record in the diaries he kept regularly, filling thirteen volumes until his death in 1898. There is no such entry. But the diaries for the years 1858 to 1862 are missing, so a visit may have occurred during that period. But the house built for Dean Liddell was not ready for occupation until 1865, says one sceptic. He is corrected by another source who says the Liddell family first occupied it in 1862. Nevertheless, can absent diaries serve as conclusive evidence that he ever—or never—visited Pen Morfa? Curiouser and curiouser, since Alice's marriage to Reginald Hargreaves was not recorded in the Diary, perhaps it is unfair to assume that Dodgson entered every important event.

However, we have the evidence of Alice herself: at the age of eighty, she recalled with great pride his visits to their

Llandudno home and their games in the sandhills. Did she remember accurately? Can her memory at that venerable age be trusted? Further testimony is offered by another first-hand account. Sir William Richmond painted a portrait of the three Liddell daughters ('The Three Graces') which now hangs in the Tate Gallery. He recalls that Lewis Carroll wrote part of *Alice in Wonderland* at Pen Morfa and remembers his reading the story aloud in the evenings to family and guests assembled there.

Sceptics can spoil all sorts of good stories—like the picnic to Godstow, with all the participants confirming that the weather was glorious. An appeal to the Weather Bureau has disclosed adverse conditions for that date—'cool and rather wet' with an inch of rain!

There is no doubt that the house of the Liddells, then called Pen Morfa, is now part of the Gogarth Abbey Hotel. Dodgson's presence—ghostly, legendary or otherwise—is real, for the house is certainly associated with Alice. It is still a monument capable of giving pleasure to many. Why spoil a good story? Moreover, it might even be true! The hotel serves as a valuable literary link, even if we apply the logic so succinctly stated by Tweedledee in *Through the Looking-Glass:* ' "Contrariwise," continued Tweedledee, "if it was so, it might be; and if it were so, it would be; but as it isn't, it ain't. That's logic". '

THE MIDLANDS

★ ★ ★

HENRY JAMES

★ ★ ★

at

THE RANDOLPH HOTEL
BEAUMONT STREET
OXFORD

Oxford is the same old Oxford still . . . We
spent a large portion of yesterday strolling
from college to college and from garden to
garden and the pleasure was great.

Letter to his parents from the Randolph Hotel,
4 June 1872

Like typical tourists today, Henry James made Oxford a stop
on his itinerary, but Henry James was no ordinary traveller. In
the first year of his life—he was born in New York City on
15 April 1843—the James family went abroad and young
Henry learned to walk and talk in England. He returned
several times with his restless family to the European scene
and kept returning continually to travel, to study and,
ultimately, to live in England.

In 1869 he made his first adult trip abroad and spent eleven
weeks in England before going on to the Continent. He was
to call it his 'passionate pilgrimage'. In England, he went in
search of castles, ruins or sites with literary associations.
He visited such places as Malvern, Leamington, Tintern
Abbey, Worcester, Tewkesbury, Salisbury and Winchester.
Oxford was a particular favourite. In a letter of 26 April, to
his brother William, he called it an 'incomparable town' and
went on to describe an evening walk he made to Christ
Church to deliver a letter, 'It was a perfect evening and in the

[163]

interminable British twilight the beauty of the whole place came forth with magical power...' He was invited to dine at several of the college halls, and he especially enjoyed various college gardens. He wrote of the gardens, 'They are places to lie down on the grass in forever, in the happy belief that the world is all an English garden and time a fine old English afternoon.'

So overwhelmed was he with his visit to Oxford that a letter he wrote from Venice to William the following September contains this initial reaction, 'I personally prefer Oxford; it told me deeper and richer things than any I have learned here.' Another letter from Venice to a friend expresses his love for the mother country: 'The more I see of the Continent, the more I value England.'

Although a cautious spender, he did not deny himself the comforts of a good first-class hotel when on his travels. In Oxford, he put up at the best—the Randolph Hotel.

The Randolph Hotel, built in 1864, was quite new when Henry James stayed there. The dark brick, Victorian Gothic style edifice, now a four-star hotel owned by Trusthouse Forte, is still the best and most luxurious in Oxford. Located in the heart of the city just opposite the Ashmolean Museum, it is ideally situated for visiting and 'strolling from college to college'. In addition to 109 guest bedrooms, which vary in size and decor, the hotel offers the height of luxury and extravagance in the Balliol and Trinity suites, named for two of the nearby colleges. The dining room offers tempting cuisine, and a coffee shop and bar extend their services to guests. In the splendid and relaxing lounge are served those delicious cream teas for which the area is known.

No wonder Henry James returned to the Randolph when he returned to Oxford in the summer of 1872. On that occasion he was acting as escort for his sister Alice who was making her grand tour with Aunt Kate, part of the James household. The group went from Liverpool, where the ship docked, to Chester, where they stayed at the Queen Hotel. Years later, Lambert Strether of *The Ambassadors* stayed at this hotel in Chester.

Henry James
(1843–1916)
stayed at the newly
built Randolph
Hotel when he
made his first visit
to England and
Oxford

Henry James wrote home from Oxford of their progress: the threesome had travelled to Derbyshire ('scenery . . . strangely raw and vacuous'), Lichfield ('truly divine Cathedral'), Warwick and Leamington ('most lovely'), before reaching Oxford. While 'doing' Oxford, they made a detour to nearby Blenheim Palace: 'It is all more lordly and lovely even than when I saw it before.'

The group went on to London, then to the Continent—France, Switzerland and Italy. At the end of the tour, after seeing Alice and Aunt Kate safely ensconced on board their ship in Liverpool for the return voyage, James stayed on in Europe to test his determination to become a financially independent writer.

About two years later, at the age of thirty-one, he began to prove himself. He had earlier tried his hand at writing with some success. He had produced travel pieces, stories, and a longer work of fiction which appeared in the *Atlantic Monthly* in 1871; *Watch and Ward*, an indication of the greatness to come, was revised and published years later in book form.

In 1875 he published a volume of his collected short stories about Americans abroad called *A Passionate Pilgrim and Other Tales*. In the title story, the characters wander through Oxford and give the author an opportunity to describe his beloved city with its 'hoary college walls' and 'antique stillness'. That year also saw the appearance of a book of travel articles, *Transatlantic Sketches*, and the novel *Roderick Hudson*—an auspicious start for the author of such masterful novels as *Washington Square*, *The Portrait of a Lady*, *The Spoils of Poynton*, *The Turn of the Screw*, *The Wings of the Dove* and *The Golden Bowl*.

The year 1875 also marked the start of his life as an expatriate. He wrote from London in a letter dated in November: 'I take possession of the old world—I inhale it—I appropriate it!'

He was eventually to appropriate Lamb House in Rye, the house with which he is generally associated and in which he lived from 1898 until his death in 1916. But he was lionised in

London before he retired to Rye. He felt comfortable and content with London and delighted in its connections with Dickens, Thackeray, Defoe, Dr Johnson. For nine years he resided in Bolton Street in Mayfair, a short street with Green Park at one end and Curzon Street, where Becky Sharp lived, at the other. It pleased him to think of his immediate neighbourhood as belonging to the character created by Thackeray. Early in 1886 he left the small, dark rooms of his Mayfair quarters and installed himself in a bright, large, fourth-floor flat with a view, in De Vere Gardens, Kensington.

He became a well-known literary figure, particularly after the success of *Daisy Miller* in 1878, and was much in demand socially. During the middle years, as he called this period of his life, he wrote such mature novels as *The Bostonians*, *The Aspern Papers*, *The Lesson of the Master* and *The Princess Casamassima*.

His books were warmly praised by the critics but not purchased in substantial quantities by the public: although he was a critical success, he was not a great financial success. In the 1890s, the respected author, the cosmopolitan artist, ventured into the theatre in the search for a more lucrative outlet. He hoped that a drama of his would overtake the London stage, but he experienced the most devastating failure of his life.

On the opening night of his play, *Guy Domville*, 5 January 1895, the nervous author attended a performance of Oscar Wilde's *An Ideal Husband* in an attempt to make the tense hours pass quickly. As he listened to the laughter of an audience that was being given the frivolous entertainment it wanted, he must have had a premonition of the fate that awaited his own serious play with its unhappy ending.

Guy Domville was an instant disaster. As the play was drawing to a conclusion, George Alexander delivered the line, 'I'm the last, my lord, of the Domvilles' and a voice from the gallery loudly responded, 'It's a bloody good thing y'are.' The audience howled and hooted, and general chaos reigned at the end of the play. When actor-manager George Alexander came out to restore order, adding at the end of his brief speech of apology that the company would try to do better in the future, another voice shouted, "'Taint your fault guv'nor, it's a rotten play.' The sensitive author fled from the scene of his humiliating failure.

He was given some encouragement in several decent reviews; particularly kind was the critic for the *Saturday Review*, George Bernard Shaw. But a career as a dramatist was essentially over for Henry James. This is especially ironic when we consider that Henry James, who spent his life considering the ironies of life, has written scores of fictional works that have been adapted into successful and effective productions for stage, cinema, television and even opera.

Needing to get away from the fiasco, James travelled to Ireland, then returned briefly to London before again escaping to the Osborne Hotel in Torquay, Devonshire. Although Torquay was simply too far from London, his positive response to it made him feel the advantages of a country retreat and gave him the idea which led to the purchase of his dream house in Rye.

Henry James left London for the Sussex country retreat which derives its name from Mayor James Lamb who built it in 1723. Now owned by the National Trust, Lamb House is open to visitors, who come in droves to see the home of the legendary master. In his own time, guests came in droves to see Henry James. He was hospitable to a partial rollcall of such names as Edmund Gosse, H. G. Wells, Joseph Conrad, Stephen Crane, Ford Madox Ford, George Gissing, G. K. Chesterton, Rudyard Kipling, Max Beerbohm and Edith Wharton.

From Rye, he did not travel so much as he did in his younger London years, but the inveterate traveller did continue to go out in search of interesting sites, people and ideas. One of his obsessive ideas found expression in *The Jolly Corner*. That tale concerns an American expatriate who, after a period of thirty years abroad, returns to New York in search of himself—the self that might have been had he

remained at home. It is a haunting and frightening auto-
biographical idea, a journey into the self. But for Henry James
there was no alternative. He had to fulfil his destiny as a writer
living in Europe.

In all of his travels, Oxford ranks high. In his decision to
reside in England, Oxford again ranks high, for Henry James
had written of it, 'The whole place gives me a deeper sense of
English life than anything yet.'

★ ★ ★

NATHANIEL HAWTHORNE

★ ★ ★

at

THE SWAN
BIRD STREET
LICHFIELD
STAFFORDSHIRE

. . . an old-fashioned hotel, its street-front
being penetrated by an arched passage, in
either side of which is an entrance-door to the
different parts of the house, and through
which, and over the large stones of its
pavement, all vehicles and horsemen rumble
and clatter into an enclosed court-yard, with a
thunderous uproar among the contiguous
rooms and chambers.

Our Old Home

Nathaniel Hawthorne was nearly fifty when he first came to
England, his first time abroad. He had already written his
great works—*The Scarlet Letter* (1850), *The House of the
Seven Gables* (1851) and *The Blithedale Romance* (1852). But
one minor work, a campaign biography of Franklin Pierce,
his old friend from Bowdoin College, earned for him a reward
after Pierce was elected fourteenth President of the United
States in 1853—the position as American consul at Liverpool.

Acceptance of this political plum for a term of four years
would give him financial security and fulfil his desire to see
old England and the roots of his ancestors. He left New
England, which had been his home from the time of his birth
on 4 July 1804, to live with his wife and three children in
Liverpool, then a major port for British exports to America.

The consulship proved to be a difficult assignment and
Liverpool, an unattractive city. But he escaped whenever he

[170]

Nathaniel Hawthorne (1804–1864) stayed at The Swan, Lichfield, to pay homage to Dr Johnson's memory could and wandered through the country in order to see as much of Britain as possible.

Hawthorne kept a journal from the spring of 1853 when he arrived in England to the early winter of 1858 when he left for Italy. He had hoped to produce a work of fiction out of his English experience but succeeded only in producing *The Marble Faun* out of the Italian experience which followed.

Nevertheless the influence of the English experience can be seen in later works. A notebook entry tells of a beautiful Jewish girl who sat opposite him at one of the many banquets he was required to attend as consul; she became the model for Miriam in *The Marble Faun*. In *Doctor Grimshawe's Secret*, Hawthorne might be recalling his own feelings as the young hero leaves his native land for his English ancestral home on a visit that 'seemed to him like a coming home after an absence of centuries'.

Hawthorne did no creative writing during the four years of his consulship, but he did find time for his journal, trying, as he said, to 'keep a tolerably full record of my travels.' He succeeded admirably, for his notes amounted to some three hundred thousand words. He covered a great deal of territory and a great number of pages.

After returning to the United States in 1860, he constructed from his journal notes *Our Old Home*. The volume was published in 1863 and dedicated to the man responsible for the years in England, the unpopular ex-President.

The following year, Hawthorne took an excursion with Pierce in the New Hampshire hills. He had not been well and hoped to regain his health on this recuperative holiday, but he died suddenly in a little place called Plymouth on 19 May 1864 at the age of sixty. His plans to return to England never materialised.

Our Old Home is filled with records of his holiday excursions and impressions of England and the English. It is filled with keen observations as he makes his jaunts through Britain. He visited such nearby places as Chester, Wales and

Shrewsbury. And he went farther afield to cities and towns including Salisbury, Warwick and Woodstock. He took a pilgrimage to Boston, Lincolnshire. He visited London often and wrote Hogarthian descriptions of its slums and investigated precincts that reminded him 'of some of Dickens's grimiest pages.'

He particularly enjoyed visits to places with literary associations. In Scotland, he went to Sir Walter Scott's Abbotsford and to the haunts of Burns. A visit to Byron's Newstead Abbey was also on the itinerary. He was somewhat disappointed with Stratford and said of his visit to Shakespeare's house that he had 'not the slightest emotion while viewing it.' But the Lake District of Wordsworth he described in superlative terms: 'I question whether any part of the world looks so beautiful as England—this part of England, at least—on a fine summer morning.'

Dr Johnson held a special place in his heart, for Hawthorne felt closer to Dr Johnson and other Augustans than he did to Shakespeare and the Romantics. He had written about Johnson earlier in a series of biographical sketches for children and was still intrigued by the episode in which Dr Johnson stood bareheaded in the rain in the market place as penance for having disobeyed his father some fifty years earlier. Hawthorne referred to his visit to that scene from the life of Johnson as 'one of the few purely sentimental pilgrimages that I ever undertook.'

It seems that he gave himself the Johnson pilgrimage as a birthday treat, for the date of the visit as given in the journal is Wednesday, 4 July 1855—his fifty-first birthday.

The chapter of *Our Old Home* entitled 'Lichfield and Uttoxeter' is a tribute to Samuel Johnson. Hawthorne writes of the journey to Lichfield 'partly to see its beautiful cathedral, and still more . . . because it was the birthplace of Dr Johnson.' In Lichfield he found the cathedral very striking with its 'peaks and pinnacles and the three battlemented towers, with the spires that shot heavenward from all three, but one loftier than its fellows . . . A Gothic Cathedral is surely the most wonderful work which mortal man has yet achieved, so vast, so intricate, and so profoundly simple . . .'

He describes the peaceful cathedral close surrounded by houses belonging to church dignitaries, and he singles out the one in which Addison must have lived when his father was Dean of Lichfield. Within the section on the close, he incorporates his primary reason for taking the tour: 'Johnson must have been familiar with it, both as a boy, and in his subsequent visits to Lichfield, an illustrious old man.'

Hawthorne continued his sightseeing tour of Lichfield with a visit to the house in which Johnson was born, now the Samuel Johnson Birthplace Museum. Michael Johnson built the house a year or two before his son Samuel was born in 1709, and he carried on his bookselling trade in the large room on the ground floor. At the house, Hawthorne consciously placed his hand on the balustrade and his foot on the steps 'where Johnson's hand and foot must many a time have been.'

Hawthorne ventured forth on his perambulations from a hotel in the centre of Lichfield. In the journal entry of 4 July 1855 he first erroneously gives the name of the Lichfield hotel at which he stayed as the Red Lion, then corrects his error explaining, 'I had made a mistake about the name of the house: it was not the Red Lion, but the Swan, and had a picture of a Swan (black, if I remember right) hanging before it.' But by the time he came to transcribe his notes for *Our Old Home*, he did not 'remember right' and said that he 'put up at the Black Swan' in Lichfield.

There never was a Black—or Red—Swan at Lichfield, and his description of the simple Swan accords with the renovated building that is today the oldest surviving coaching inn in Lichfield. Perhaps Hawthorne confused it with another hotel where he stayed, the Black Swan in York; or with the Swan in Newby Bridge where the family enjoyed a holiday that same month; or was he perhaps thinking of Liverpool which became for him a 'black and miserable hole'?

Yet another possibility for his insertion of blackness into the name suggests itself in his continuing description of the

[174]

interior with its 'great, dull, dingy and dreary coffee-room'.
Feeling the 'ponderous gloom' he 'buried' himself 'in a huge
heap of ancient feathers . . . and slept a stifled sleep . . . And
when I awoke, the musty odor of a bygone century was in my
nostrils.' In any case, after 'a very good supper, and good
breakfast, dinner, and sherry,' he went on to Uttoxeter the
next day to find the exact spot where the famous Dr Samuel
Johnson, the great writer and producer of the Dictionary, did
penance for having refused to take the place of his ailing
father at the Uttoxeter bookstall. Disappointment is reg-
istered over the fact that no memorial marked the spot:

How strange and stupid it is, that tradition should not have
marked and kept in mind the very place! How shameful
(nothing less than that) that there should be no local
memorial of this incident, as beautiful and touching a
passage as can be cited out of any human life . . . Such a
statue, if the piety of the people did not raise it, might
almost have been expected to grow up out of the pavement,
of its own accord, on the spot that had been watered by the
rain that dript from Johnson's garments, mingled with his
remorseful tears.

Moreover, the locals seemed to know nothing about the very
incident which had so moved him.

Nevertheless, his visit to the Swan of Lichfield and to
places associated with Johnson was a successful one.
Fortunately, the city of Lichfield still has a great deal of
interest to show to its present-day tourists, including the
ancient St John's Hospital which dates to Tudor times, as
well as the ancient Swan itself.

The Swan dates back to the early 1500s. It has thirty-two
bedrooms and an interior with oak beams and simple
furnishings. The Lichfield Official Handbook of 1906
described the Swan as, 'a comfortable Family Hotel, overlooking the Cathedral, and near Dr Johnson's House, one of
the old-fashioned country inns so beloved by tourists.' The

description needs no updating. (Alongside the car park at the rear, in the former stable block and cockfighting pit, a new wing of eight bedrooms is unobtrusive.)

The original Swan is a rambling coaching inn with many levels and steps—steps down to the dining room, up to the meeting room, up and down to some of the bedrooms, with no uniformity of shape or dimension in any of the rooms. Some rooms are tucked into the eaves, and exposed old beams from dismantled ships are part of the decor. Occasional notices warn 'Mind Your Head' or 'Mind the Step'.

Examination of the maze of corridors divulges spaces behind walls that are unaccounted for. Perhaps these were priest holes and hidden passageways. And there is no accounting for the non-existence of Rooms 1 and 2. At least the friendly ghost in residence is authentic, and the lady in white, formerly a barmaid, is seen regularly by members of the staff.

In particular, Room Number 4 must be singled out: a plaque over the low door announces, 'Dr Johnson Slept in this Room.' What a pity that Hawthorne was not apprised of that information! A boldly-patterned carpet in tones of yellow, gold and olive covers the sloping floor which inclines upward across the room to the window with a cheery view of the garden and the cathedral's three spires. Two modern and comfortable beds, no ancient feathers, offer repose. But ancient oak beams in the bathroom are complemented, fortunately, by modern fixtures. A clever builder could have straightened the floors and walls and re-shaped the building —and spoiled it all.

More oak beams enhance the cosy dining room with its oak tables and chairs and its dominant, but disused, brick fireplace fitted with black iron stove.

A newly refurbished bar, its eighteenth-century panelled walls hung with photographs of old Lichfield, takes its name from the large scene over the fireplace, 'The Prospect of Lichfield'. A drink in this pleasing environment might be ordered in the words of George Farquhar, author of *The*

Beaux' Stratagem, written in 1707 in the George Inn just over the road in Bird Street:

I have heard your Town of Lichfield much fam'd for ale,
I think I'll taste that.

Visible from Bird Street is the outline of the now-enclosed 'arched passage' of the Swan through which coaches would have driven on their way into the stable yard at the rear. Above, sits a three-dimensional white swan, not on a nest, but on the letters H-O-T-E-L.

A convenient centre for city sightseeing, the hotel also makes a fine geographical centre for further literary exploration—George Eliot's Nuneaton or Arnold Bennett's Five Towns around Stoke-on-Trent.

One good literary pilgrimage deserves another. Just as Hawthorne deliberately tried to walk in the footsteps of his beloved Dr Johnson, so the visitor to the Swan might step where Nathaniel Hawthorne walked in 1855 while on *his* pilgrimage.

at

PERRY HALL HOTEL
BROMSGROVE
HEREFORD AND WORCESTER

That is the land of lost content
I see it shining plain,
The happy highways where I went
And cannot come again.

A Shropshire Lad

When Alfred Edward Housman, the eldest child of Edward and Sarah Jane Housman, was only a few months old, the family moved into Perry Hall in Bromsgrove. Alfred was born in the Valley House in Fockbury, just two miles from Bromsgrove. It was to the Valley House that Edward had brought his bride after their marriage in 1858, and in that house Alfred was born on 26 March 1859. For a brief period the Housmans lived there, just a few hundred yards away from the Fockbury home of Edward's parents, where Edward had spent his boyhood.

At Perry Hall, the Housman family grew. Another child, Robert, was soon born, followed by Clemence and then Katherine. A fifth child, Basil, was followed by a sixth, Laurence. And when Alfred was nine, the last child, George Herbert, was born to the prolific couple. But Sarah Jane's health began to decline, and happy days at Perry Hall were soon to be over. Nevertheless, the house and its surroundings had a shaping influence on the young poet.

The large garden of Perry Hall was the place for childish play where imagination was allowed to run rampant. There was a flowering cherry tree, a vegetable garden, and a secluded rubbish garden filled with fruit trees. Chestnut trees were

A E Housman
(1859–1936) and his
childhood home,
Perry Hall,
Bromsgrove, now a
hotel

planted in the garden, one for the birth of each new child. The seven children enjoyed a happy time of sunshine days. They each had their own climbing tree and were full of invention and creativity. Even then Alfred showed a delight in words and a talent for writing. His brother Laurence was to become a poet and playwright, the author of the well-known play, *Victoria Regina*. By the time he was fifteen, Alfred was already a published poet: while a pupil at the Bromsgrove School, his *Death of Socrates* won a prize in a school competition and appeared in *The Bromsgrove Messenger* in August 1874.

The tower and spire of Bromsgrove Church could be seen from Perry Hall. Naturally, church attendance was compulsory and the sound of church bells became an integral part of their lives. The bell which rang at one o'clock on Sundays (for no known reason) was dubbed 'the Yorkshire-pudding bell'. The poet was later to use bells quite often in his writing, *Bredon Hill* being perhaps his most popular bell poem:

> In summertime on Bredon
> The bells they sound so clear;
> Round both the shires they ring them
> In steeples far and near,
> A happy noise to hear.

Those happy days lasted until Alfred was about ten. His mother was discovered to have cancer and her health began to fail. Edward was simply unable to cope with her deteriorating state and with financial problems—mortgages and interest payments. He withdrew, he took to drink for escape from his problems. The sensitive Alfred suffered severely and was sent to stay with relatives, where he would avoid the painful scenes. There, on his twelfth birthday, he received word of the death of his mother.

After Sarah Jane's death, Edward married a cousin, Lucy Housman, who was much loved by all the children. To escape from a house full of memories, Edward took advantage of an opportunity to leave Perry Hall and move two miles away, back to his boyhood home in Fockbury. The Clock House, also known as Fockbury, was the family home where Edward's parents had lived while his father was vicar of the new church in the parish of Catshill.

Fockbury House, the new home of the Housmans, was surrounded by the open countryside and by views of the distant Shropshire hills in contrast with the enclosed garden of Perry Hall. But Laurence Housman wrote in his autobiography, *The Unexpected Years,* that the Fockbury House was 'never as intimately our home as Perry Hall had been.' The young Alfred habitually walked alone, enjoyed the beautiful landscape, and meditated on the hills which later became a romantic symbol, as expressed in his *Last Poems:*

> From hill and cloud and heaven
> The hues of evening died;
> Night willed through lane and hollow
> And hushed the countryside,
> But I had youth and pride.

> And I with earth and nightfall
> In converse high would stand,
> Late, till the west was ashen
> And darkness hard at hand,
> And the eye lost the land.

An unsuccessful lawyer, Edward Housman planned to use Perry Hall as offices, but he had no income to support his life style. Indeed, financial problems plagued him for the rest of his life. When continuing difficulties caused the sale of Fockbury House in 1877, the family returned to Perry Hall. This was also the year when Alfred left Bromsgrove for Oxford, having won a scholarship to St John's College.

Further financial mishandling of affairs brought the family dangerously close to complete ruin. At one point, in February 1879, Edward's youngest brother, the Reverend Joseph

Housman, bought Perry Hall and allowed Edward to stay on, rent free. Edward dealt with the worsening situation by continuing to drink his way into oblivion.

Alfred came home to Perry Hall for several visits, sometimes with Oxford acquaintances. One in particular, A. W. Pollard, was to become a life-long friend. What an enormous strain the old familiar rooms and gardens must have been to him, since the poor family could not even afford now to keep a fire going.

Having done poorly at Oxford, possibly because of emotional problems and involvements, he passed Civil Service examinations and took a position as clerk in the London Patent Office where he worked for ten years. Meanwhile, he continued his classical studies reading Greek and Latin in the British Museum, and he began to publish articles and papers. Scholarly work and translations continued and his scholarship paid off. In 1892 he became Professor of Latin at University College, London. He made up for his youthful failure at Oxford by becoming a great and respected scholar in the classics. When an application for a post at Cambridge University was successful, he moved in 1911 to Trinity College for another twenty-five years as Professor of Latin.

But during his nineteen years in London, when he lived alone in Highgate, he began the writing of much of his serious poetry. Eventually, the volume by which he will always be known, A Shropshire Lad, was published in 1896. Originally called The Poems of Terence Hearsay, the change of title (suggested by Pollard) helped to ensure its success. Perhaps the Terence of A Shropshire Lad, named for the Greek dramatist who was brought to Rome as a slave, parallels Housman's own feeling of exile in London from his childhood home.

Although Alfred had written since childhood, the poems that flowed from his London pen are imbued with the spirit of his boyhood places and with a sense of irretrievable and poignant loss. There is a strong sense of reaching out for remote and idealised places which he once possessed, but which exist now only in his memory. He got geographical facts wrong and later admitted that details of topography were unimportant to him. He mentions actual places such as Ludlow and Wenlock, but Shropshire came to symbolise the unknown, the land of dreams.

As a child, he had walked a great deal and taken in the view to the west of the distant Shropshire hills. But—and this is the astonishing fact—Shropshire was never his home and he spent very little time there. His Shropshire landscape, together with its inhabitants, belongs to the poetic imagination. It does not have the solidity of, for example, Wordsworth's Lake District.

A Shropshire Lad had been rejected by several publishers before it finally appeared at the poet's expense. It got off to a slow start but quickly grew in appeal and reputation. Many of the poems of later volumes were actually written before *A Shropshire Lad* but were withheld from publication until a later date because of their personal nature. By the time *Last Poems* appeared in 1922, Housman was established as the most popular English poet after Kipling.

As for his former home, with the family gone, and with the death of his father in 1894, there was no point in retaining Perry Hall. Alfred came home for his father's funeral, and the sad memories are reflected in a later poem:

> Around the huddling homesteads
> The leafless timber soars,
> And the dead call the dying
> And finger at the doors.
>
> Oh, yonder faltering fingers
> Are hands I used to hold;
> Their false companion drowses
> And leaves them in the cold.

Perry Hall survived, together with its garden and cherry tree and surrounding countryside, in reality as well as in

Housman's poems. The seven chestnut trees were transplanted along the graveyard wall of Catshill Church. His ashes were buried in the heart of Shropshire, in Ludlow. There, in the churchyard of St Laurence, a simple plaque announces: 'In memory of Alfred Edward Housman, MA Oxon, Kennedy Professor of Latin and Fellow of Trinity College Cambridge. 1859-1936.'

But the reference to his poetry is all around—from the purple crocuses in front of the plaque:

> I heard the beechnut rustle down,
> And saw the purple crocus pale

to the cherry tree which still stands in the grounds of Perry Hall:

> Loveliest of trees, the cherry now
> Is hung with bloom along the bough.

Perry Hall was built by John Adams, the great-uncle of Edward Housman, in 1824. He purchased the site for his powder and dye factory and retained the name of the original ruined mansion for the fine new house distinguished by neo-Gothic windows and vast front door. The solid house had a number of pleasantly furnished large rooms, high frescoed ceilings, wide marble fireplaces, huge kitchen and an altogether elegant and restful atmosphere. It lay at the foot of Adams' Hill (named for the man who also built the sloping path and steps in the hill on which the church stands) in Kidderminster Road (for the road leads northwest to the town of Kidderminster).

Perry Hall remained a private residence until 1952, spent a brief period as a private club, and then became a hotel in April 1956. Although the interior has been greatly altered, it still has the original fireplace (in what is now known as the Clent Room), stained glass and oak panelling. Its rooms now serve as offices, conference rooms, restaurant, ballroom and lounge-bar. A large portrait of Alfred Edward Housman hangs in the lounge. The new owners, Embassy Hotels, added an extension in 1969 to give the hotel fifty-five bedrooms. The unobtrusive new wing is separated from the main house by a corridor.

But the exterior has been preserved. Even the front door is the original. The Gothic windows and ivy-covered façade make a dignified impression. A plaque proudly commemorates the Housman connection. Outdoors, in fine weather, it is possible to enjoy the enclosed garden with its famous cherry tree which is still thriving. Guests can sit around the small white tables which have been tastefully arranged in the garden. There they may contemplate the past, perhaps with refreshments from the bar which opens up into the secluded garden. There it becomes appropriate to recall the cynical words of Terence Hearsay:

> Say, for what were hop-yards meant,
> Or why was Burton built on Trent?
> Oh, many a peer of England brews
> Livelier liquor than the Muse,
> And malt does more than Milton can
> To justify God's ways to man.
> Ale, man, ale's the stuff to drink
> For fellows whom it hurts to think:
> Look into the pewter pot
> To see the world as the world's not

Perry Hall supplies all kinds of memories of a 'land of lost content' while its cellars, fuller now than they were for Edward Housman, supply something more tangible.

Edward Housman often indulged at the nearby Golden Cross or Shoulder of Mutton. At the Shoulder of Mutton, just over the road in St John Street, the burden of supplying him with drink fell on the shoulders of the landlord. Several prominent notices on the front of that public house give the salient facts of the connection. In particular, one panel announces, 'The poet's father Edward used to hurl a stone on to a tin roof at Perry Hall as a signal for the Landlord to go to him jug in hand.' All of Bromsgrove is proud of the Housman connection, and many visitors repair to this public house, said to be the oldest in town, for its nostalgic offerings.

In the year of the birth of Alfred Edward Housman, Bromsgrove was a small market town with a long history. It is mentioned in The Domesday Book as Bremesgrave and was important enough to be granted a Fair Day by King John. Now it is important enough to be a Midland town with light industry and some of the surburban overspill of Birmingham. Growth and so-called progress is inevitable, and a fine fifteenth-century merchant's house was among those scheduled for demolition in 1962 to make way for a huge supermarket. But the dwelling was rescued, and five years later it was re-erected in the nearby Avoncroft Museum of Buildings, where it can be visited along with such other rescued structures as a counting house, barn, granary, cockpit theatre and windmill. Yet, many find old buildings still remain in Bromsgrove including the sixteenth-century grammar school, the Church of St John the Baptist with fourteenth-century tower and spire, some attractive Georgian houses in the High Street—and Perry Hall.

For further offerings to Housmania, the pilgrim could imbibe in the non-mythical Shropshire scene, taking in the places which he uses in his poetry: Ludlow (with its eleventh-century castle), Bredon, Shrewsbury and the ancient market towns of Much Wenlock and Bridgnorth (which he visited when he was staying at Perry Hall after his father's death).

In addition to the Perry Hall Hotel, two other Housman houses in the neighbourhood are extant—Fockbury House where Edward and Lucy Housman lived with the children for six years and the Valley House in Fockbury, now known as Housmans, where the poet was born.

From far, from eve and morning
And yon twelve-winded sky,

[186]

The stuff of life to knit me
Blew hither: here am I.

In a very real sense, much remains of various A. E. Housman
associations not only reachable but also well worth reaching.

★ ★ ★

GEORGE ELIOT

★ ★ ★

at

GRIFF HOUSE HOTEL
NUNEATON
WARWICKSHIRE

> There is no sense of ease like the ease we felt
> in those scenes where we were born, where
> objects became dear to us before we had
> known the labour of choice, and where the
> outer world seemed only an extension of our
> own personality: we accepted and loved it as
> we accepted our own sense of existence and
> our own limbs.

> *The Mill on the Floss*

Some thirty miles north of Stratford, in the same county which has become a mecca for Shakespeare devotees, is the home of one of the great novelists of all time. Mary Anne Evans was born in Warwickshire on 22 November 1819. When she died in London on 22 December 1880, she was well known as the respected and great author, George Eliot.

Robert Evans, land agent for the Newdigate family of Arbury Hall, was the head of a family consisting of the two children of his first marriage and the three children of his second marriage to Christiana Pearson in 1813, Christiana, Isaac and Mary Anne. When Mary Anne was four months old, the Evans family moved from the house called South Farm in which she was born to another house on the Arbury estate, the more spacious and attractive Griff House. Griff was to be her home for the next twenty-two years.

Now, well over a century later, Griff House looks very much as it did in those early years of George Eliot's life, years that she always recognised as extremely important, as ex-

[188]

George Eliot (1819–1880). Griff House, near Nuneaton, was her home for the first 22 years of her life and formed some of the background to *The Mill on the Floss*

pressed in *Daniel Deronda*. 'A human life, I think should be well rooted in some spot of a native land . . . a spot where the definiteness of early memories may be inwrought with affection.'

It is with affection that one may visit the red brick house and look for haunting signs of George Eliot's presence. Little has changed. The present dining room was the dining room then. The bow window projects out from the drawing room. The attic window above the drawing room is still visible, and the attic retreat in which Maggie of *The Mill on the Floss* 'fretted out all her ill-humours, and talked aloud to the worm-eaten floors and the worm-eaten shelves' is now a private retreat for the owner of the hotel. If further reminders are needed, a plaque has been built in over the front door announcing, 'GEORGE ELIOT lived here March 1820 to March 1841.'

The Griff House Hotel is a middle-priced hotel with twenty-four rooms, nine in the original house and fifteen in the new wing. Most rooms have private baths, and all have television and tea-making facilities. The restaurant offers an excellent range of food from bar snacks to complete menus.

The Griff House Hotel, a pleasant place to visit, is also an extremely important place because George Eliot had her 'childhood in it' and 'accepted and loved it as we accepted our own sense of existence and our own limbs.'

Located on the Coventry Road just a mile and a half from Nuneaton, Griff House is not situated in the most inspiring or beautiful landscape of England. Nevertheless, its setting delighted children with a pleasant garden for play, a pond and a canal, barns filled with cows and the resultant happy task of butter- and cheese-making. The youngest child enjoyed a tranquil, uneventful and apparently happy childhood. She was particularly fond of her brother Isaac, who was three years older, and the two were inseparable. A sonnet-sequence called *Brother and Sister* which she wrote from the idealised viewpoint of a middle-aged woman recalls childhood:

The bunched cowslip's pale transparency
Carries that sunshine of sweet memories,
And wild-rose branches take their finest scent
From those blest hours of infantine content.

She returned often to this place of 'infantine content' in her writings.

Enjoyable diversions came when Mary Anne accompanied her father on his rounds as he collected rents or attended to business affairs. She took in her native countryside as well as her father's commentary and later recalled those drives in *Middlemarch:*

> . . . through a pretty bit of midland landscape. . . . Little details gave each field a particular physiognomy, dear to the eyes that have looked on them from childhood: the pool in the corner where the grasses were dank and trees leaned whisperingly; the great oak shadowing a bare place in mid-pasture; the high bank where the ash-trees grew; the sudden slope of the old marl-pit . . . the huddled roofs and ricks of the homestead . . . the grey gate and fences . . . the stray hovel, its old, old thatch full of mossy hills and valleys with wondrous modulations of light and shadow. . . . These are the things that make the gamut of joy in landscape to midland-bred souls—the things they toddled among, or perhaps learned by heart standing between their father's knees while he drove leisurely.

The feeling of belonging and vitality associated with the midlands area is summarised in *The Mill on the Floss:*

> We could never have loved the earth so well if we had had no childhood in it—if it were not the earth where the same flowers come up again every spring that we used to gather with our tiny fingers as we sat lisping to ourselves on the grass . . . What novelty is worth that sweet monotony where everything is known, and *loved* because it is known?

The two children of that novel bear close resemblance to Mary Anne and Isaac Evans and Dorlecote Mill was based, at least in part, on Griff House. The long attic in which the Tulliver children played has its counterpart in the one which runs from one end of Griff House to the other: 'Maggie was already out of hearing, making her way towards the great attic that ran under the old high-pitched roof . . . This attic was Maggie's favourite retreat on a wet day, when the weather was not too cold . . .'

Other elements of the geographical setting appear in other books. The vegetable and flower garden at the rear was probably the Hill Farm garden of *Adam Bede,* and the garden walk was that which led to the summer house at Lowick Manor in *Middlemarch.*

When Isaac was sent away to school, his doting sister took to reading voraciously, and they grew apart. (Indeed, her scandalous union with George Lewes many years later was to cause a permanent rift between brother and sister.)

When her mother died in 1836, Mary Anne was made responsible for the running of the house. Five years later Mr Evans retired; Isaac carried on as land agent and moved with his bride into Griff. Mary Anne continued to care for her father when father and daughter moved to a house known as Bird Grove which still stands at Foleshill at the edge of Coventry.

A stubborn freethinker, Mary Ann—she discarded the 'e'— incensed her irate father when she also discarded her religion and refused to accompany him to church. He disowned her. She returned in ignominy to live for a while with Isaac and Sarah at Griff House.

Her father died in 1849. The breach was not entirely healed, and it must have been extremely painful to her to find that he had left the set of Scott's novels, from which she had often read aloud to him, to her half-sister.

Marian (as she now began to call herself) decided to travel on the continent for a while before settling into a new life in London. She moved into the home of publisher John Chapman, whose *Westminster Review* she helped to edit, and there she met such notables as Charles Dickens, Wilkie Collins and Florence Nightingale. She also met George Henry Lewes with whom she fell deeply in love; but archaic laws prevented him from securing a divorce from his adulterous wife, once he had acknowledged her child by another. George Eliot daringly consented to live openly with this man in a bond that was to last nearly twenty-five years, until his death in 1878. It was he who encouraged her to write the fiction which she produced under the pen name of George Eliot, a name chosen because 'George was Mr Lewes's Christian name, and Eliot was a good mouth-filling, easily-pronounced word.'

She worked hard on translations and reviews but had always wanted to write fiction. Novels, she calculated, would be even more lucrative than the esoteric and intellectual journalism she was producing. Her first story was *Amos Barton*, the first of a series of stories to be called *Scenes of Clerical Life*.

This was followed by the first full-length novel, *Adam Bede*, published in 1859. A journal entry of 16 November 1858 cites Griff House as the source for that novel as she relates an anecdote told by her aunt, which became the germ for the novel: 'We were sitting together one afternoon during her visit to me at Griff, probably in 1839 or 1840, when it occurred to her to tell me how she visited a condemned criminal . . .'

The Mill on the Floss which followed in 1860 had strong autobiographical elements, recalling in particular her closeness to her brother Isaac, now alienated from her because of her shocking and disgraceful union with Lewes. Success was immediate and other novels followed: *Silas Marner* (1861), *Romola* (1862), *Felix Holt* (1866), *Middlemarch* (1871) and *Daniel Deronda* (1876).

A year after the illicit but happy union came to an end with the death of Lewes, her last work, a volume of essays called *The Impressions of Theophrastus Such* (1879), was published.

An infatuated old family friend proposed to her when she was sixty and, after much deliberation, she accepted John

Walter Cross, twenty years her junior, as her husband. The marriage was to last just six months. The year was 1880, the year of her death.

Although never considered pretty, George Eliot must have been an extremely lovable person, full of warmth and sincerity. Bret Harte wrote of her, 'Her face lights up when she smiles . . .' No, she was not beautiful in the conventional sense of the word, but what an attractive and endearing spirit —what inner beauty—must have been hers! Perhaps the visitor to Griff House can sense some of her extraordinary qualities in this 'spot of a native land' that was once part of George Eliot.

at

HAMBLETON HALL
HAMBLETON
OAKHAM
LEICESTERSHIRE

Mrs Cooper lived at Hambleton in Rutland,
about three miles from Oakham in the middle
of Cottesmore country. The village stands on a
hill rising abruptly out of chequered fields,
polite and green and neatly hedged.

Present Indicative

When he was fifteen, Noël Coward accepted an invitation to
stay at Hambleton Hall, the home of Mrs Astley-Cooper. The
invitation came at the instigation of Philip Streatfield, an
artist with a studio in Chelsea, whom Noël had met the
previous year when he was fourteen and Philip was about
thirty. They became good friends.

Philip could not imagine the effect that the country air of
Hambleton and the wisdom of Mrs Cooper would have on the
lad. The visit, which took place in June 1915, was to have a
profound influence on Noël Coward's future life and career.
Hambleton was Noël's introduction to comfortable country-
house life, complete with fox-hunting. He thoroughly
enjoyed and profited from Mrs Cooper's style and wit, and the
visits to her taught him to be completely at ease with the
upper classes, whether with them or writing about them.

Mrs Cooper was a delightfully eccentric hostess given to
spouting words of wisdom from a supine position before the
fire. She became a long-time friend, and Noël saw her at many
other times and venues. On a later visit to Hambleton Hall, he
entertained soldiers when it was being run by Mrs Cooper as a

[195]

convalescent hospital during the war. In the spring of 1919, he performed at village concerts, impressing the local audience with his professional London status. Sometimes he sang with Mrs Cooper's daughter, Phyllis. He recalls the treasured experience in his autobiography, *Present Indicative:*

Small memories are the most insistent, and I like to catch again, for a moment, the feel of the sharp spring air as we drove home at night after a concert, the smell of the wood fire in the library where we discussed, over hot soup and sandwiches, the triumphs of the evening. All the warm, comfortable ingredients of country-house life were there, the very unfamiliarity of the atmosphere enhancing its charm for me . . . This, I reflected, quite wrongly, was my rightful sphere, and I would go upstairs to bed, undress, and brush my teeth, still, until sleep closed down upon me, accurate in my performance of a country gentleman.

On later holidays, he joined Mrs Cooper in Italy at Alassio, and he stayed with her at Cap Ferrat on the Riviera.

At Hambleton he found and read a volume by Saki which further helped to mould in his own mind the technique to use in writing about Edwardian country-house affairs—how to express its atmosphere and charm by use of wit. Without question, his friendship with Mrs Cooper and his visits to Hambleton Hall helped to shape his career, a career which could only have been with the stage.

His destiny began to form not many years after his birth, on 16 December 1899. He was taken regularly to the theatre from the age of five. At seven, he performed in amateur productions and made his professional debut as a child actor in *The Goldfish* in January 1911. Engagements continued throughout life, and acting became a means of advancing theatrical and literary ambitions.

He learned every aspect of the theatre. After the opening of *The Young Idea*, in February 1923, he was noticed as a brilliant young playwright. A writer of great promise, he had

Nöel Coward
(1899–1973) first stayed
at Hambleton Hall,
former home of Mrs
Astley-Cooper, at the age
of 15, and made frequent
visits later

promised himself while still in his teens that he would become famous and rich and this he proceeded to do. By 1925 he had completed three plays which firmly established him as a dramatist: *The Vortex, Fallen Angels* and *Hay Fever.* A first-rate playwright, he was also an actor, director and composer of merit who freely incorporated song, music and dance into his plays. International fame was his by 1926.

In the golden years from 1928 to 1934 came his great successes as a writer: *This Year of Grace, Bitter Sweet, Private Lives, Cavalcade, Words and Music* and *Design for Living.* Virginia Woolf wrote in a letter to Noël of *This Year of Grace,* 'Some of the numbers struck me on the forehead like a bullet. And what's more I remember them and see them enveloped in atmosphere—works of art in short.'

His writing tends to lash out at hypocritical society and denounce smug Victorian attitudes. He saw into the absurdity of the human condition. Often in his plays, one character represents integrity and clarity and thus Coward's own attitude. He can be flippant and laugh away cares, but he can also be serious and see into the heart of things. Enjoyment of life runs through his writing. In *Private Lives,* Elyot expresses to Amanda his zest for living: 'Let's blow trumpets and squeakers, and enjoy the party as much as we can, like very small, quite idiotic school children. Let's savour the delight of the moment. Come and kiss me, darling, before your body rots, and worms pop in and out of your eye sockets.'

Behind the frivolous dialogue of the characters is a sadder, wiser and more serious theme. Elyot and Amanda cannot live together because of clashes of ego, and they cannot live apart because of their love for each other. They are honest and intelligent and aware of their situation, which is after all the absurdity of the human condition.

The plays of the 40s include the superbly entertaining *Present Laughter,* in which a group of people fall in and out of love with one another, and *Blithe Spirit* which again uses a romantic triangle to get at the reality of such human emotions as jealousy.

[198]

In the mellowed phase of his later life, he wrote such plays as *Relative Values, Quadrille* and *Nude with Violin. Look after Lulu* is an adaptation of a Feydeau farce. *Waiting in the Wings,* the last of his full-length plays, takes place in a home for old and retired actresses.

His plays range from farce to serious drama. He revived the comedy of manners, as sophisticated people are caught in comic situations. With techniques of satire, irony and wit, bad behaviour is held up to ridicule and the loss of chivalrous values is deplored. But behind the fun, there is always the assertion of life, not a cynical denial of it. Even the patriotic *Cavalcade* leaves one with the feeling that, despite tragedy, life is worth living.

Some of his plays have been relegated to literary oblivion, but he remains a popular writer with a prolific and varied output. He also wrote a novel *(Pomp and Circumstance),* several volumes of short stories, travel books and a book of verse. *In Which We Serve* is a fine film and a good piece of wartime propaganda. He followed up his first autobiography, *Present Indicative,* with another, *Future Indefinite.*

He was knighted in 1969 and awarded an Honorary Doctorate of Letters from the University of Sussex in 1972. When he died suddenly at his Jamaican home on 26 March 1973, he left behind a vast number of plays with enduring and endearing qualities which will keep him in the forefront as one of the wittiest English playwrights ever.

As long as mad dogs and Englishmen go out in the midday sun, as long as the Mrs Worthingtons of the world try to put their daughters on the stage, Noël Coward's praises will be sung. Good fortune makes it possible for us to return to the site of the early inspiration and expression of his prodigious talent.

Located on a peninsula in a large reservoir called Rutland Water, Hambleton Hall is set in an enchanting position. It is a large Victorian mansion surrounded by acres of gardens and sheer beauty, in the county formerly known as Rutland, now Leicestershire.

The present owners are Tim and Stefa Hart, who have converted it into a small hotel. Fifteen bedrooms are individually decorated and furnished in traditional style. The drawing room is luxurious and the bar so pleasant and cosy that the visitor may neglect the gorgeous outdoor scene.

Noël 'grandly descended the polished oak staircase' and guests who emulate that proud action are in for a particular treat as they too descend for dinner. The elegant hotel restaurant boasts of a young English chef who trained at Maxim's in Paris and creates inspired dishes at Hambleton.

Cared for with such love and dedication, Hambleton Hall offers guests the high standards of country-house living so adored by Noël Coward. Above the door of the house is the Rabelaisian motto: *Fay ce que voudras* or 'Do as you please.' The owners promise a warm and friendly welcome. They do not guarantee that fame and fortune will follow, but with such a precedent already established, anything is possible.

EAST ANGLIA

CHARLES DICKENS

at

THE GREAT WHITE HORSE HOTEL
TAVERN STREET
IPSWICH
SUFFOLK

In the main street of Ipswich . . . stands an inn
known far and wide by the appellation of The
Great White Horse, rendered the more con-
spicuous by a stone statue of some rampacious
animal with flowing mane and tail, distantly
resembling an insane cart-horse, which is
elevated above the principal door. The Great
White Horse is famous in the neighbourhood,
in the same degree as a prize ox, or county
paper-chronicled turnip, or unwieldy pig—for
its enormous size.

Pickwick Papers

Charles Dickens is associated with more geographical
locations than almost any other author and slept in more
places than George Washington. In Broadstairs alone, where
he wrote *Nicholas Nickleby* and *Bleak House* among others,
so many plaques abound attesting to his residence within,
that one plaque facetiously points out that Dickens did *not*
live there. His job as a journalist gave him many
opportunities to visit a variety of places.

Although born in Portsmouth on 7 February 1812, in a
house which is now a Dickens Museum, his happy childhood
years were spent in Kent. The family moved to Chatham
when Charles was five, and he explored thoroughly the
Kentish area all around, including nearby Rochester. He

roamed through town and dockyard, watched ships sailing down the Medway out to sea, and examined Rochester's Norman cathedral and its ruined castle. He sometimes took long walks with his father in which they climbed the long hill to ramble through Cobham woods, ending up by Gad's Hill, scene of Falstaff's revels. There they admired the rose-brick country house known as Gad's Hill Place.

He wrote about all these places in his books, thereby immortalising them. In later life he returned rich and famous and able to purchase the very house he had coveted, Gad's Hill Place, where he lived for the last twelve years of his life until his death on 8 June 1870.

But for the young boy, his years in London meant misery. In the winter of 1822 the family moved to the city where the struggle with poverty was unremitting. When his father was arrested for debt and thrust into a debtors' prison at Marshalsea, Southwark, in February 1824, Charles was thrust into manhood. He could not continue his schooling; he bitterly resented the work he did at Warren's Blacking Factory (later described in *David Copperfield*) pasting labels on to bottles of the factory's product in a rat-infested warehouse by the river for a few shillings a week. He felt betrayed and humiliated and abandoned. Eventually, through a small and lucky legacy, the debt was paid, and John Dickens took on work as a political reporter while his son resumed schooling.

With a strong need now for success and security, Charles became a clerk in a firm of solicitors and at the same time emulated his father by learning shorthand. He mastered the system in less than a year, and the skill enabled him to do freelance legal reporting in courts known as Doctors' Commons, no longer in existence. He took down every word in the cases assigned to him and transcribed his symbols into reports, and he would sometimes use even the most trivial incidents in his own writings.

After two years he became a newspaper reporter for the *True Sun*, then for the *Mirror of Parliament*. He recorded speeches made in the House of Commons and reproduced

Charles Dickens
(1812–1870) used
The Great White
Horse Hotel,
Ipswich, in
Pickwick Papers

them verbatim. His speed and accuracy led to his appointment within two years as political reporter for the prestigious *Morning Chronicle*.

Meanwhile, he wrote short pieces for the *Monthly Magazine* and the *Morning Chronicle* to which he appended the pseudonym 'Boz'. One of the sketches contains a description of Doctors' Commons, 'where they grant marriage-licences to love-sick couples and divorces to unfaithful ones, register the wills of people who have any property to leave, and punish hasty gentlemen who call ladies by unpleasant names.' The collection was published in volume form as the *Sketches of Boz*. Years later, references to Doctors' Commons appeared in *Pickwick Papers, Oliver Twist, David Copperfield* and *Master Humphrey's Clock*.

With his first attempt at authorship, he was well on the way to becoming a great writer. The year was 1836, the year also of his marriage to Catherine Hogarth. Charles Dickens himself took out a marriage licence at Doctors' Commons.

He was to become a brilliant literary artist as well as a concerned and compassionate human being. Exploration of London's slums and of England's factory towns made him work and write to help victims of industrial civilisation by calling attention to their plight. The marriage was to be an unhappy one which filled his life with domestic misery, although he remained attached to his children. But his rise to the highest literary position in the land was meteoric, and by 1848 he was an international celebrity.

As a young journalist on the staff of the *Chronicle*, he was sent out into the provinces to report on elections and political speeches. Fortunately, he loved travel. Coaches and coaching inns became part of his way of life, a life which shows up as pretty little scenes on tin biscuit boxes or on greeting cards but which is actually not so romantic as those scenes would have the onlooker believe. But the young reporter did find excitement and invigoration in the change of vistas, and he found an opportunity for adapting his experiences to his writing purposes.

His impressions, full of accurate observations and originality, ultimately found an outlet as he wrote a stage coach
traveller's view of the country starring Mr Pickwick. Printed
in monthly parts, this revolutionary practice in publishing
engaged a large reading public attracted to the often hilarious
experiences of his amusing characters, especially Sam
Weller. The episodic *Pickwick Papers* of 1837 launched his
immensely successful career as a novelist. Shortly thereafter
came *Oliver Twist, Nicholas Nickleby, The Old Curiosity
Shop* and *Barnaby Rudge*—five books in five years.

As a traveller, Dickens seems to have relished in particular
the welcome produced by a good inn for the guest who, after
the hardships of a wearying or cold coach ride, is in great need
of the comforts of a blazing log fire and good food and wine in
a friendly atmosphere. He knew a variety of inns and appreciated the character and individuality of each. From the
decrepit public houses to the smart hotels—he wrote about
them all in his diary, in his letters and in his books. And
because he mentioned them, they became famous.

He described his travels and the inns he frequented with
his reporter's discriminating eye for detail and with honesty,
both for the comforts and the discomforts. He describes the
George in Grantham, where he went to gather material for
Nicholas Nickleby, as 'the very best inn I have ever put up at.'
But he was rather unkind to the Great White Horse in
Ipswich, where he went in 1835 to report on the Suffolk
elections at Ipswich and Sudbury. The opportunity supplied
him with his Eatanswill of *Pickwick Papers* and gave him the
material for his novel.

Travellers receive their first impressions of an inn and
judge it initially by outer appearance, and Dickens introduces
his readers of *Pickwick Papers* to the Great White Horse by
citing its location 'in the main street of Ipswich . . .' followed
by an impression of the exterior. Today's visitor might view
the stone statue of his 'rampacious animal' as a gentle horse
who acts as a jolly signboard to indicate the name of the haven
to be found within.

[205]

After maligning the façade, Dickens goes on to castigate the menu and the service which greeted the new arrivals: 'After the lapse of an hour, a bit of fish and a steak were served up to the travellers, and when the dinner was cleared away, [they] . . . ordered a bottle of the worst possible port wine, at the highest possible price . . .'

Dickens must have known the interior of the inn well for he wrote in *Pickwick Papers:* 'Never were such labyrinths of uncarpeted passages, such clusters of mouldy, ill-lighted rooms, such huge numbers of small dens for eating or sleeping in, beneath any one roof, as are collected together between the four walls of the Great White Horse Inn.' His Mr Pickwick gets into difficulty because of the rambling geography of the inn which thoroughly confused him when he tried to retrieve the watch he had left downstairs: 'The more stairs Mr Pickwick went down, the more stairs there seemed to be to ascend, and again and again, when Mr Pickwick got into some narrow passage, and began to congratulate himself on having gained the ground-floor, did another flight of stairs appear before his astonished eyes. . . . Passage after passage did he explore; room after room did he peep into . . .'

He recovered his watch but not his way back and entered the wrong bedchamber where he found himself sharing the bedroom of a strange lady with curl-papers in her hair: 'Mr Pickwick almost fainted with horror and dismay. Standing before the dressing-glass was a middle-aged lady, in yellow curl-papers, busily engaged in brushing what ladies call their "back-hair".'

Dickens stayed at the Great White Horse for several weeks, and the experience of being in the wrong bedroom may well have been his own. That might explain his prejudice and his criticisms. Since the white horse which highsteps over the portico is tamer than the animal he describes, perhaps his derogatory comments in general could be tamed down as well.

Dickens' comments notwithstanding, the hotel is alive and

well and thriving in Ipswich, a town located some seventy miles from London and worth a visit in its own right.

Situated on the River Orwell Estuary, it has always been a flourishing seaport. Chaucer refers to it in the Prologue to the *Canterbury Tales* when he describes the pompous Merchant of Ipswich:

> He wolde the see were kept for anythyng
> Bitwixe Middelburgh and Orewelle.

Appropriately, Dickens loved the sea and sea towns. But the heart of Ipswich today has largely lost its seafaring atmosphere. The narrow, congested streets arranged in a medieval pattern contain interesting old buildings everywhere. One particularly fine architectural example is the Ancient House in the Buttermarket, a gorgeous example of an ornate plasterwork decoration characteristic of East Anglia and known as 'pargeting'. Amidst the interesting old buildings is the centrally-located hotel which makes the most of the Dickens association.

The inn, well over four hundred years old, has the charm of age. Thanks to the efforts of the Dickens Fellowship, this galleried inn has been preserved with the remains of the timber-framed courtyard inside. And carpets instead of cobblestones contribute to the comfort of the feet and to the inviting, pleasant atmosphere.

The Great White Horse Hotel treasures a connection which would be envied by the grandest of hotels. It proudly capitalises on the faults Dickens attributed to it and uses them for advertising, showing off Mr Pickwick's bedroom where the famous adventure is supposed to have occurred. Actually, it is a fine room and even Dickens relents: 'It was a tolerably large double-bedded room, with a fire; upon the whole, a more comfortable-looking apartment than Mr Pickwick's short experience of the accommodations of the Great White Horse had led him to expect.'

Everywhere are Pickwick pictures and the Pickwick spirit.

Yes, the hotel does have tortuous passages, no doubt more noticeable because of Mr Pickwick's experience. Furthermore, meandering corridors and staircases are typical of any English hotel with a history.

Such notables are supposed to have stayed here as King George II and Admiral Nelson and Lady Hamilton, but the words written by Dickens give him the dominant association and give the hotel immortality. With such a background, the hotel will no doubt continue to thrive without ever losing the modifier of its title—'Great'!

LORD BYRON

---

at

SWYNFORD PADDOCKS
SIX MILE BOTTOM
CAMBRIDGESHIRE

For thee, my own sweet sister, in thy heart
I know myself secure, as thou in mine;
We were and are—I am, even as thou art—
Beings who ne'er each other can resign . . .

Epistle to Augusta

'Try everything once,' said Sir Thomas Beecham, 'except incest and folk dancing.' It is not known whether Byron ever tried folk dancing.

When Byron and Augusta met in 1813 in London, the attraction was strong and mutual. The graceful couple quickly became steady companions and shared a busy social life. To an outsider, the situation might have seemed to contain all of the elements of a perfect romance. Never mind that she was twenty-nine and five years older than he. Never mind that she was married. Or that she had three children. The problem was that they were brother and sister.

Augusta's mother died shortly after she was born, and Augusta was brought up in the care of her maternal grandmother, Lady Holderness. In 1785 her father remarried, and her half-brother George Gordon Byron, born on 22 January 1788, was the son of that second marriage. 'Mad Jack', as their father was known, died when Byron was three.

Brother and sister grew up apart and shared none of the ordinary experiences of siblings. They had met earlier, but his mother discouraged contact with Augusta. They had corresponded, but exchanges became infrequent from 1807 when she married her cousin, Colonel George Leigh, and ceased in 1809 when he left on his grand tour—his Childe Harold's Pilgrimage.

Back in England after his two-year sojourn, communication between Augusta and Byron resumed with her letter of sympathy on the death of his mother. He was a sensational overnight success with the publication of the first two cantos of *Childe Harold* and became the lion of London society. Augusta was full of curiosity about her 'baby Byron'. They arranged to meet.

Hers was not a happy marriage. Her wandering and worthless husband was a selfish egotist, a spendthrift and a gambler, who was always in financial difficulty. Appointed equerry, Colonel Leigh managed race horses at Newmarket for the Prince of Wales, who gave him the conveniently-located house in the hamlet of Six Mile Bottom. He was usually busy at the races and away from home. Left alone with her three small children, Augusta felt neglected and bored. On a visit to a friend in London, she and Byron met and found that they shared not only the same father but a deep affection, which was to grow into a permanent and passionate love.

They spent most of the summer of 1813 together, and Byron made several visits to her Cambridgeshire home. He followed her to Six Mile Bottom within a few days of her departure from London. After his second visit, he persuaded her to come back with him to London. That summer they decided to remain together always and planned to flee to the Continent. Lady Melbourne, his confidante, who was privy to the escape plan, helped to dissuade him, saying that it was a 'crime for which there was no salvation in this world, whatever there might be in the next.'

Byron's regular visits to Six Mile Bottom continued. He often wrote outside in the summer garden under a huge tree which came to be known as 'Byron's tree' but, alas, not destined for the kind of immortality alloted to Milton's mulberry in Cambridge. Byron's beech was felled some twenty years ago and only the rise in the ground from the huge roots remains. He worked here on *The Corsair*, a tale of

Lord Byron (1788–1824) and
Swynford Paddocks, where
he lived with his half-sister
Augusta Leigh

incestuous love, with Medora, a name later chosen for Augusta's fourth child, as one of the characters. The hero, a 'man of loneliness and mystery,' was identified by many as the author:

> He left a Corsair's name to other times,
> Linked with one virtue, and a thousand crimes.

Their love continued unabated, and in January of the following year, Byron took Augusta to his ancestral Newstead Abbey home, just as any loving husband might give a pregnant wife a holiday break. There they were alone and extremely happy —and snowbound for ten days. They carved their names on a tree. There is no doubt that they adored each other. The blissful holiday over, she returned to Six Mile Bottom; he, to London. He visited her again in March, then returned the following April when Elizabeth Medora Leigh was born. The Colonel was away in Yorkshire, but Byron came to Six Mile Bottom to be with her.

They both agreed that he should take the expedient step of securing a wife. Marriage would deflect gossip. After proposing to Annabella Milbanke, he was again at Six Mile Bottom. His impending marriage seemed doomed before it took place. He hesitated about going to see Miss Milbanke, and he hesitated about the marriage. But the wedding finally took place on 2 January 1815. That date enabled him to spend the preceding Christmas with Augusta.

The honeymoon was dreadful and the aftermath was worse. The newlyweds were Augusta's guests at Six Mile Bottom for some two weeks in March. His behaviour towards his wife was cruel from the beginning. He humiliated the young bride by sending her to bed early, indicating that he preferred his sister's company. He hinted strongly at his incestuous affair. He once pointed to Medora and announced that she was his own child.

Augusta returned the visit to the Byrons in April and stayed at their fashionable London address, which was filled with domestic strife. Annabella left him after their child Augusta Ada was born in December. She tried to have her husband certified insane. Augusta was dragged into the scandalous proceedings, which ended in a deed of separation in April 1816. On the 23rd of that month, he left England, having said good-bye to Augusta a week earlier. Abroad, 'the wandering outlaw of his own dark mind' turned to his poetry. Augusta continued to occupy his thoughts, and his poems include the *Epistle to Augusta:*

> My sister! my sweet sister! if a name
> Dearer and purer were, it should be thine;
> Mountains and seas divide us, but I claim
> No tears, but tenderness to answer mine:
> Go where I will, to me thou art the same—
> A loved regret which I would not resign,
> There yet are two things in my destiny,—
> A world to roam through, and a home with thee.

But he was destined never to see his beloved Augusta—or England—again. He travelled to Switzerland and Italy, where he produced among other works, the third and fourth cantos of *Childe Harold, Don Juan, Beppo, Manfred* and *Mazeppa.* He set out in 1823 to join the Greek insurgents in their fight for freedom and died of fever in Missolonghi, Greece, on 19 April 1824.

Byron's biography contains many unsolved problems. While it may never be known with absolute certainty that Byron slept with Augusta, it is certainly known that he slept in Augusta's home in Six Mile Bottom.

The Byron spirit still lives in that house, formerly known simply as the Lodge. Renamed and remodelled, it is now a country-house hotel called Swynford Paddocks. It sits at the end of a long drive amidst large trees in pleasant grounds. With gabled roof and prominent chimneys, and with attractive greenery which partly covers the white exterior, it still gives the impression of a large private house.

The present proprietor admits that his purpose in purchasing the property with some forty acres of paddocks was to make it a profitable stud. The hotel aspect came as something of an afterthought. But what started as a comfortable home for the owner with a few rooms for guests has become a comfortable house for guests, with the owner residing in a smaller house elsewhere in the grounds.

The approach to Swynford Paddocks from London, fifty-eight miles to the south, passes through the hamlet with the suggestive name of Six Mile Bottom. Actually, the name derives from the fact that it stands in a hollow six miles from Newmarket.

This area of England, famous for horses and horse-racing since the time of Charles II who loved the sport, offers a variety of activities. If walking around the stud results in boredom there is the possibility of visiting the Newmarket racecourse. There is always the lovely countryside to be enjoyed by taking drives, as did Augusta, across the Devil's Dyke to the town of Newmarket or over the Gog Magog Hills with their prehistoric Iron Age hill-fort of Wandlebury Ring. Cambridge is just nine miles away, and stately homes such as Anglesey Abbey are open to the public. But one can just as easily stay indoors and imbibe the Byron atmosphere of Swynford Paddocks.

Tastefully decorated throughout, the lounge is furnished with antique pieces. The twelve bedrooms are extremely comfortable and supplied with such amenities as fresh flowers, colour television and books. The management displays great awareness of the scandalous scenes played out in its premises well over a century and a half ago. Huge, dominating portraits of Byron, Augusta and Medora hang on the staircase wall. Among the books in the bedroom is a biography of Medora Leigh, *Byron's Daughter;* the guest may choose between sin or sanctity, biography or bible, for bedtime reading.

The restaurant offers culinary excellence with a liaison of English and French dishes. Wines too are distinguished, and a few are unique, including a pleasant English wine from nearby Ely known as Etheldreda.

Swynford Paddocks dispels dark and gloomy accusations of dreaded incest in its bright, cheerful and elegant atmosphere. Those able to create their own canto for a private pilgrimage are in for a treat. Byron travelled in style. It is fitting that those who follow his travels can do so stylishly at Swynford Paddocks.

THE NORTH OF ENGLAND

―――――――――――――――――――― ★ ★ ★ ――――――――――――――――

AGATHA CHRISTIE

―――――――――――――――――――― ★ ★ ★ ――――――――――――――――

at

THE OLD SWAN
HARROGATE
NORTH YORKSHIRE

This next little fact—no! Ah, that is curious!
There is something missing—a link in the
chain that is not there.

The Mysterious Affair at Styles

How Agatha Christie came to write is no mystery, for she tells
it in her autobiography. A challenge from her older sister ('I
bet you can't write a good detective story'), together with her
love for story telling, produced in 1915 what has been called
'one of the finest firsts ever written', *The Mysterious Affair
at Styles*. From the time it was published in 1920, the prolific
Agatha produced at least a book a year. 'A sausage machine, a
perfect sausage machine', she has called herself.

A great deal of mystery surrounds a particular episode in the
life of Agatha Christie when the lady vanished, only to be
discovered eventually at a Harrogate hotel. One essential clue
to her disappearance, which reveals something of her nature,
might be that, with a penchant for titles that intrigue, she
chooses for the story of her life a title that could hardly be
simpler—*An Autobiography*—and she omits any mention of
her stay in Harrogate. The silence is deafening; the mystery
deep. Why the use of the indefinite article? Why the omis-
sion? It is as if she shuns calling attention to herself as anyone
very special. Yet, the case does not call for the uncanny

Agatha Christie
(1890–1976) in old age.
In 1926 the lady
vanished, only to be
discovered in Harrogate
Hydro, now The Old
Swan Hotel

OLD SWAN HOTEL
(FORMERLY HARROGATE HYDRO)

abilities of a Hercule Poirot to solve the riddle and uncover the facts which make up the account of her disappearance.

Agatha Miller and Archibald Christie were married in 1914 and divorced in 1928. In 1926 she was under considerable strain brought about by the death of her mother, the pressures of constant work, and the impending breakup of her marriage. That year, on the evening of 4 December, she left her house in a highly emotional state, after learning that her husband had left for the home of his mistress, and she drove off; her abandoned car was found in Surrey with absolutely no trace of the driver.

A search for the missing Agatha ensued. As if dealing with one of her own bizarre plots in which the author became the unlucky victim, the public suspected foul play. Headlines screamed. One newspaper offered a reward. Policemen and amateurs scoured the countryside for clues. A nationwide search ended with the tip that she was at the Swan Hydro in Harrogate. It was revealed that she had in fact been staying there for nine days under an assumed name, the name of the woman who was later to become Colonel Christie's second wife. The disclosure made sensational news. The press capitalised on it. The public, perhaps feeling resentful and cheated by a non-tragic, anticlimactic outcome, claimed it was all a publicity stunt. Actually, it was most likely a case of amnesia.

Agatha Christie was a shy and modest person who always valued her privacy. When the disappearance of her happiness proved more than she could cope with, her mind ordered her own disappearance.

Why Harrogate? Why not! The author once said that the best way of getting down to work is in a very bad hotel where there is nothing else to do but write, for there are no distracting comforts to indulge in, no good meals or interesting guests. But she was not there to write when she sought refuge at a very good hotel in Harrogate. In fact, she was an entertaining and charming guest whose engaging personality was enjoyed by those present. She even played the piano with the orchestra and seemed to be having quite a happy holiday in Harrogate.

The possibility for a happy, salubrious holiday is the reason for the existence of Harrogate in the first place. The history of the elegant spa town begins when the insignificant hamlets of High and Low Haregate were destined to become a new and important town after a chalybeate (iron) spring, called Tewit Well, was discovered there in 1571. Discoveries of other mineral springs followed. With the publication in 1626 of a book by Dr Edmund Deane extolling the virtues of the mineral spirits, crowds began to pour in to try out the recommended waters of the Old Sulphur Well. Daniel Defoe visited in 1724 and wrote of a pleasant time in this 'desolate out-of-the-World Place'. But the place became more and more worldly.

Accommodation had to be provided for the enthusiastic hordes who followed the enthusiastic reports of many physicians, and the historic and elegant Old Swan Hotel was built in the beginning of the eighteenth century to provide for the fashionable clientele.

Constructed of Yorkshire stone, the Old Swan retains its dignity in a town located two hundred and eight miles from London, a town which has become a centre for tourism and conferences now that the fashion for taking the waters has declined. Nevertheless, the elements of the spa town are still there to be seen and enjoyed—the Royal Baths Assembly Rooms, the prettily-domed Tewit Well, the many gardens, the long glass-covered walk known as the Sun Colonnade, the Royal Hall and the Royal Pump Room, which now serves as a museum and supplies samples of the smelly sulphur water which started a social trend.

The grand four-star hotel offers excellent service, good food and one hundred and thirty attractive rooms, many with garden views. It offers also the atmosphere of a stately home with its Red Lounge containing a baronial fireplace and with its beautiful Garden Room Suite. In paying tribute to the past, it does particular honour to one famous literary guest by its naming of the Agatha Christie Library Restaurant.

The hotel's situation near the Yorkshire Dales presents an endless array of attractions to explore. But when Agatha Christie was found there in 1926, she was exploring inner needs, and she was afterwards able to return to a normal and productive existence.

In 1930, Agatha Christie married the archaeologist Max Mallowan, after which she began a happy life which included her appointment, in 1971, as Dame of the British Empire. She died in 1976 at the age of eighty-six.

During her hard-working life, she produced over eighty titles, contriving to have her eightieth title appear on her eightieth birthday. Her books are enormously popular and are outsold only by the Bible and Shakespeare. Her films and plays are equally successful with *The Mousetrap* (which opened in 1952) setting a worldwide record as the longest running stage play ever. Her books, translated into over a hundred foreign languages, are known around the world.

The detective story may be considered an ephemeral literary form, and critics may ponder the reasons for her vast success and permanence. But it does not require the skill of Hercule Poirot muttering about his little grey cells to solve this mystery: Dame Agatha creates a puzzle full of suspense and supplies a satisfying solution which restores order to a chaotic world. Simply, she offers a good read.

WILKIE COLLINS

at

THE ROYAL HOTEL
WEST CLIFF
WHITBY
NORTH YORKSHIRE

Eastward was the grey majesty of the sea,
hushed in breathless calm; the horizon line
invisibly melting into the monotonously
misty sky; the idle ships shadowy and still on
the idle water.

No Name

A born storyteller, William Wilkie Collins was born in London on 8 January 1824. He was apprenticed to a firm of tea importers at the age of seventeen, later studied law, and even appeared on stage as an actor. But he was always interested in writing, and his sketch called *The Last Stage Coachman* was published when he was nineteen and still in the tea business. He eventually made the decision to devote himself to writing as a profession.

The writing career of Wilkie Collins spans forty years and shows a yield of over twenty novels as well as novelettes, short stories, essays and plays. But the large output of this popular Victorian novelist contained only two novels which have achieved status as classics, *The Woman in White* and *The Moonstone*.

His first book was a debt to his father, a successful landscape painter who died in 1847 leaving his son with the obligation of producing a biography. His journal contained words construed as a command: 'I think it quite possible that my dear son, William Wilkie Collins, may be tempted, should it please God to spare his life beyond that of his father, to furnish the world with a memoir of my life . . .' *Memoirs of the Life of William Collins, Esq., RA* was published in two volumes in 1848. The biography is disappointing to today's readers because so little is revealed about the author, who kept himself out of his father's picture.

In 1851 Wilkie Collins met Charles Dickens, who became a great friend. Dickens was then forty years old, and the friendship lasted until the death of the older man some twenty years later. Completely overshadowed by his friend, Collins wrote for *Household Words*, the periodical which Dickens had founded in 1850. They collaborated on stories which appeared in that publication as well as in *All the Year Round* which succeeded it. They went on holidays together on the Continent and in Britain. A walking tour in Cumberland made by the two in 1857 became a joint writing venture for *Household Words* in which it appeared as *The Lazy Tour of Two Idle Apprentices*.

Antonina was Wilkie Collins' first novel. Its reception at the time of publication in 1850 was full of critical and popular praise. There followed a series of novels and short stories in the 1850s, largely unknown today. But *Basil, Hide and Seek* and *The Dead Secret* are a few of the commendable titles. *The Frozen Deep*, a drama of 1857, gave Dickens the idea for *A Tale of Two Cities*. Then *The Woman in White* began to appear in serial form in November 1859 and appeared in book form in 1860. It made Collins a celebrity. One envious rival publisher called it 'the most popular novel of the century'.

No Name, which followed in December 1862, tells an exciting story and deserves a better fate than the state of neglect to which it has been relegated. *Armadale* (1866) is another adventurous novel which T. S. Eliot commended for having 'every merit that melodrama can have' and for 'being never dull'.

Of his works of the 1860s, *The Moonstone* (1868), an immediate and perennial success, has been singled out as the first English detective novel, and Dorothy L. Sayers has called it 'probably the very finest detective story ever written'.

Wilkie Collins
(1824–1889) and
the Royal Hotel,
Whitby, where he
went to stay with
Caroline Graves,
the original
'Woman in White'

Charles Dickens paid the ultimate compliment by emulating it in *The Mystery of Edwin Drood*. Trollope was also influenced by it in his *The Eustace Diamonds*.

After 1870 Wilkie Collins' health, as well as the quality of his writing, declined. He was tortured by an illness diagnosed as rheumatic gout and became addicted to opium taken as a palliative for pain. The 'all-powerful and all-merciful drug' had been discussed by Dr Ezra Jennings of *The Moonstone*.

Despite his agony, Collins continued to write and remained a popular novelist, no doubt always aware of the single work which had established and maintained his reputation and popularity throughout his lifetime. After his death on 23 September 1889, these words were inscribed, according to his own directions, on his tombstone in the Kensal Green Cemetery: 'Author of *The Woman in White* and other works of fiction.'

Such are the basic facts of the literary life of Wilkie Collins. The facts of his private life are more difficult to ascertain. Collins was reluctant to allow his private life to become public knowledge. His close friends respected his wishes and remained silent. Many letters were destroyed, and certain biographical details were omitted from contemporary accounts. His life style was unconventional, indeed shocking, and could only be condemned by Victorian standards of morality.

In 1859 Collins met Caroline Elizabeth Graves with whom he lived for about eight years. He also formed a liaison with Martha Rudd, the mother of his three children. Caroline left and married Joseph Clow in October 1868 but returned to live with Collins in the early 1870s and remained with him until his death. She was the prototype for *The Woman in White*. The story of their meeting and how it inspired his great work is as melodramatic as anything he wrote.

Wilkie Collins and his brother Charles were accompanying their friend Millais home after a dinner given by Mrs Collins, when a piercing female shriek from a nearby villa broke the peace of the summer evening. Then the iron garden gate

[224]

opened and a beautiful young woman in white flowing drapery materialised. She paused briefly where the three men stood before running off to disappear into the moonlit night. Wilkie dashed out after the white luminescent figure and did not return to his waiting friends.

The next day, Wilkie related to his friends her story: she had been imprisoned in the Regent's Park house which the threesome happened to be passing at the time of the scream. A man, perhaps her husband, used threats, restraints or mesmerism to keep her captive. But that night, she managed to escape from the fortress and fled, pursued by Collins who reported her to be in a suicidal condition. Collins, entranced and haunted by the mysterious figure, followed her about all night to prevent harm.

Forty years after the fateful meeting, and ten years after the death of Wilkie Collins, *The Life of John Everett Millais* (1899) by J. G. Millais was published—another son fulfilling an obligation to a father. The account of the fantastic meeting with the woman in white is contained in that biography.

Further testimony is offered by the wife of Charles Collins who asserted in her old age that the distressed damsel of the Millais account was the same woman who came to live with Collins. She was Caroline, wife or widow of George Robert Graves. She was in her early twenties at the time of the meeting and had a daughter less than a year old. Caroline was to play an influential role in the life of Wilkie Collins.

Whether the incident is a product of the imagination or not, the novel of sensation which resulted was a sensational success. Collins became the famous author of a bestseller which was so popular that fashionable articles of clothing, perfumes and toilet accessories and musical compositions were named *Woman in White.*

In great demand, Wilkie Collins had already begun his next novel, *No Name,* when he decided to leave the oppressive heat of London for a pleasant seaside location. In August 1861, he took a month's holiday with Caroline Graves, staying at the Royal Hotel in Whitby. That hotel did not, however, succumb to the fad of the day by renaming itself the Woman in White Hotel.

Whitby is on the north east coast of England about twenty miles north of the more famous Scarborough. The Royal Hotel stands on the West Cliff overlooking the harbour of this fascinating old fishing port, once known for whaling. The view from the hotel also takes in the East Cliff on which stands the ruined thirteenth-century Whitby Abbey. A statue of Captain Cook, who lived in a cottage in Grape Lane near the abbey, looks out to the sea from the West Cliff which fronts on to a fine, sandy beach.

Built by the railway king George Hudson, the hotel developed a reputation for good service. It is described in *Reed's Illustrated Guide to Whitby* of 1854 as a 'splendid establishment' in which 'every attention is paid to the comfort and requirements of the visitor' and as a hotel which is 'replete with accommodations for visitors'.

Today, with six bars (including the Captain Cook Bar which pays tribute to the eighteenth-century explorer), with 135 rooms and with conference facilities, the hotel can offer a coastal resort holiday to multitudes. In August 1861 it offered a holiday to Wilkie Collins and the woman in white.

From his pleasant room overlooking the harbour and the boats, Collins worked on his novel . . . From her window overlooking the harbour, the heroine of *No Name* watches ships glide slowly by, her hand clutching a bottle of laudanum. In a state of remorse and despair, she considers suicide and determines to leave the decision to chance: If an even number of ships pass by within a half hour, she will live; if an odd number, she will take the poison. It is a highly dramatic scene as she counts passing ships against passing time:

. . . Twenty-five, twenty-six, twenty-seven, twenty-eight; and the next uneven number—the fatal Seven—glided into view. Two minutes to the end of the half-hour. And seven ships.

Twenty-nine; and nothing followed in the wake of the seventh ship. The minute-hand of the watch moved on half-way to thirty—and still the white heaving sea was a misty blank. Without moving her head from the window, she took the poison in one hand, and raised the watch in the other. As the quick seconds counted each other out, her eyes, as quick as they, looked from the watch to the sea, from the sea to the watch—looked for the last time at the sea—

Collins continued to write—that is, when he was not distracted by the noise of dozens of children including the '*fourteen* young ones' of an English matron to whom he referred as a rabbit. He was further disturbed by 'a brass band hired by the proprietor to play four hours a day.' After spending most of the month at the hotel, he made the pronouncement that 'working against noise is the hardest work of all' and returned to London. In fact, he became increasingly intolerant to noise and left his Harley Street home a few years later in search of quieter quarters.

One of his later novels, *The Haunted Hotel*, might have sufficed as a new name for the Royal Hotel which is haunted by the presence there of an important Victorian writer. The great exponent of the melodramatic tale has left us the mysteries of his stories and of his life. But there is relatively little mystery about Wilkie at Whitby.

Nor is there any mystery about his place in literary history if we take the word of T. S. Eliot who described him as a master of his genre: 'There is no contemporary novelist who could not learn something from Collins in the art of interesting and exciting the reader. So long as novels are written, the possibilities of melodrama must from time to time be re-explored. The contemporary "thriller" is in danger of becoming stereotyped . . . The resources of Wilkie Collins are, in comparison, inexhaustible.'

***

***

at

HARDCRAGG HALL
GRANGE-OVER-SANDS
CUMBRIA

The sun rose while they were crossing the
moor, a dazzle of light over the tops of the
hills. The sunshine crept down the slopes into
the peaceful green valleys, where little white
cottages nestled in gardens and orchards.

The Tale of Pigling Bland

Among the large and impressive group of famous poets and
writers associated with the English Lake District is Beatrix
Potter. Her Hill Top home in Sawrey is now a National Trust
property and is visited and enjoyed as a central symbol of her
beloved Lake District and the source of her delightful stories.

But Beatrix Potter also knew the seaside resort of Grange-
over-Sands on the southern shore of the Lake District. A
journal entry made as early as 1887 mentions a visit with her
itinerant parents to 'Grange-over-Sands on Morecambe Bay'.
The Townley family, who became good friends, lived there in
a house known as Hardcragg.

The sixteenth-century manor house then stood in open
countryside and functioned as a farm. Now the road to Hardcragg Hall Hotel goes gently uphill from the Main Street,
through a built-up area, and the view from the small white
house overlooks slate rooftops towards Morecambe Bay.

The cosy interior of the hotel, particularly when the crack-
ling log fire gives off warmth, still has original oak flooring
and panelled rooms. The panelled dining room was the
original dining room. Upstairs are eight, prettily-furnished

[228]

Beatrix Potter (1866–1943) whose piglet inspired the *Tale of Pigling Bland*

bedrooms. But how Beatrix Potter came to Hardcragg, or indeed to the Lake District, is another story.

Born in a genteel district of London on 28 July 1866 (in a house that was destroyed by bombing in 1940) Beatrix Potter learned to appreciate and love non-city life. She travelled a great deal from early childhood, as her wealthy parents were always off on holidays, always visiting or making the rounds of hotels. In the journal that she kept from the age of fifteen to thirty, Beatrix Potter made sensitive observations on such places as Exeter ('I am very fond of Exeter . . . it retains its primitive self-contained air of importance.'); Weymouth ('Much surprised by the extent and dreariness of the New Forest.'); Stonehenge ('The first view of Stonehenge is disappointing, not because it is small, but because the place whereon it stands is so immense. The stones are large enough to satisfy anybody.').

Her ability to observe and record fine detail extended to the nature studies in which she immersed herself from childhood. Together with her brother Bertram, who was five years younger, she collected fossils, skeletons and animals—dead or alive. She was committed to the study of nature. She drew and painted pictures of animals and flowers and made regular visits to the South Kensington Museum to further her studies. She was in fact an amateur naturalist. Her knowledge and skill were put to good use many years later when she came to write and to illustrate her stories.

Beatrix developed a special love for the north country and responded fully to its way of life. The rental of the turreted Victorian Wray Castle on the western shore of Lake Windermere near Hawkshead provided the opportunity for her to explore and learn about the lakes and fells of those poetic parts.

The Potters stayed in one rented property after another in their frequent summer holidays in the Lake District and were in and around the village of Sawrey several times. Lakefield (now Ees-Wyke) at Sawrey was a favourite place, and Sawrey was to become the source of her greatest fulfilment and happiness. Situated near Esthwaite Water, which she considered 'the most beautiful of the Lakes', Sawrey must have had a salubrious effect on her, for she wrote in the journal on her birthday, 'I feel much younger at thirty than I did at twenty.'

It was from the Lake District that she was encouraged to write and publish her first little book for children. The story of that book is a charming one, reminiscent of Lewis Carroll's *Alice in Wonderland,* which also began as a tale for a special child. Beatrix Potter had remained attached to her former governess even after Miss Annie Carter became Mrs Moore and the mother of a large family. When five-year-old Noël Moore fell ill and was confined to bed for months, Beatrix Potter wrote a letter to him, dated 4 September 1893, which contained a story of her rabbit Peter, enhanced by her own little pictures: 'Dear Noël, I don't know what to write to you, so I shall tell you a story about four little rabbits, whose names are Flopsy, Mopsy, Cottontail and Peter . . .'

Fortunately, Noël had kept that letter and was able to relinquish it when she decided, eight years later, to copy it, revise and enlarge it, and send it to the publishers, Frederick Warne & Company—who promptly rejected it. Undaunted, she brought out a privately-printed edition of 250 copies of *Peter Rabbit* in December 1901. The following year, she resubmitted the story—and her writing career was launched.

Other tales followed, and the earnings went toward the purchase of Hill Top Farm in the village of Sawrey, a much loved place. Another career, in farming, was launched at Hill Top with the tenant farmer staying on to act as manager or foreman. The eight years following the purchase of Hill Top were the period of her greatest creativity. She produced thirteen books, of which six are concerned with the setting, activities and people of Hill Top and Sawrey, in which she so delighted. Her children's fantasy world became extremely popular, and the financial success enabled her to buy more land.

It would be pleasant to believe that Beatrix Potter wrote her *Tale of Pigling Bland* at Hardcragg, as the hotel brochure

[231]

suggests. Looking down at the piggery from a window of an upper bedroom in which she stayed is supposed to have given her the idea for her story. Well, perhaps she did derive inspiration; perhaps Hardcragg should be credited. So what if she had her own prize-winning pigs, one of which became the prototype for the Pigling Bland character? After all, she did visit there. And another charming story attaches itself to Hardcragg:

The manager who ran the farm for Beatrix Potter often bought pedigree baby pigs from Farmer Townley. On one occasion he found himself too busy to fetch the baby pigs he had ordered. Beatrix offered to go there herself to visit the Townley farm and return with the pigs. While there, she took a liking to a tiny black female pig; but Townley refused to allow her to include it in the purchase, for it was non-pedigree. She pleaded and insisted that she would keep it apart and care for it herself. Townley had to give in. Obviously, Beatrix saw a story in it. She saw the baby pig as a companion for Pigling Bland. So Hardcragg Hall is intimately connected with the famous author. When the story was published in 1913, it was to the two Townley children that it was dedicated: 'For Cecily and Charlie, A Tale of the Christmas Pig.'

That was the year for a major change in her life. She had purchased in 1909 Castle Farm, which could be seen from Hill Top and which had a field adjoining Hill Top property. The transaction was handled by the solicitor William Heelis, and she became Mrs William Heelis in October 1913. She was forty-seven, and it was time for a change. Mrs Heelis of Sawrey was a wife, farmer and happy resident of the Lake District for the next thirty years—until her death on 22 December 1943 at the age of seventy-seven.

SCOTLAND

ROBERT BURNS

★ ★ ★

at

MURRAY ARMS
GATEHOUSE-OF-FLEET
DUMFRIES AND GALLOWAY
SCOTLAND

Scots, wha hae wi' Wallace bled,
Scots, wham Bruce has aften led,
Welcome to your gory bed,
Or to victorie.

March to Bannockburn

At the Murray Arms Hotel in Gatehouse-of-Fleet, they
proudly point out the room—the Burns Room—in which
Robert Burns composed the song that ranks with his 'Auld
Lang Syne' as one of the two most popular in Scotland. 'Scots,
wha hae wi' Wallace bled' would be the Scottish national
anthem, if Scotland had a national anthem. 'Patronised by
Robert Burns' is the claim of this small (twelve bedrooms),
charming and friendly hotel in a white-painted village about
eight miles from the ancient town of Kirkcudbright.

Places associated with Burns are legion, thanks to his
itinerant lifestyle: particularly in his corner of Scotland, the
southwest, Burns is celebrated everywhere. There is the Land
o'Burns Motoring School, the Burns Emporium, garages,
bakeries, restaurants and innumerable, inevitable gift shops.
Some adapt his poetic phrases for their names, as in 'The
Giftie Gie Us'. The cult of Burns has something of the
seriousness of a religion with a pilgrimage route known as
the Burns Heritage Trail. But in addition to places selected for

[233]

a Burns pilgrimage, the Murray Arms at Gatehouse-of-Fleet represents a stop that Burns made on a tour through Galloway.

Despite hard times, Burns managed the luxury of a week's holiday with John Syme. The two men first met in 1788 and became very close friends. Indeed, it was Syme who arranged the funeral when Burns died at the age of thirty-seven after long suffering from a heart ailment. On their tour through Galloway, the two friends made their first stop at Kenmore, where they stayed for three days before moving on to Gatehouse. They were caught in a storm and arrived at the inn wet through and railing at the elements. Burns comforted himself with drink. In the morning, his anger returned, for his boots had been badly dried and did not fit. He tore them trying in vain to pull them on and left bootless and feeling ill. Off they rode, and his good humour returned when they reached St Mary's Isle as the guests of the Earl of Selkirk.

The trip took six days and took in very little territory but produced one very important work. Syme gives this account of the tour: 'I told you that in the midst of the storm on the wilds of Kenmore, Burns was rapt in meditation. What do you think he was about? He was charging the English army, along with Bruce, at Bannockburn. He was engaged in the same manner on our ride from St Mary's Isle, and I did not disturb him . . .'

Burns was immersed in political thoughts on the ride back to Dumfries but had apparently already sketched out the words which would express the defiant fight for liberty in 'Scots, wha hae wi' Wallace bled'. The idea must have been with him for a while, for his own account is expressed in a letter of 30 August 1793 to his Edinburgh music publisher, George Thomson. He wrote that, 'the old air, *Hey, Tutti Taitie* . . . has often filled my eyes with tears.—There is a tradition, which I have met with in many places of Scotland, that it was Robert Bruce's March at the battle of Bannock-burn.—This thought, in my yesternight's evening walk, warmed me to a pitch of enthusiasm on the theme of Liberty

Robert Burns
(1759–1796) and
Murray Arms
Hotel where the
poet penned
'Scots, wha hae
wi'Wallace bled'

& Independence, which I threw into a kind of Scots Ode, fitted to the Air, that one might suppose to be the gallant ROYAL SCOT'S address to his heroic followers on that eventful morning.'

Varying accounts describing the creation of the song are further complicated by the publisher's arbitrary decision to alter the tune and modify the words to make them fit. But he wisely relented and in a later edition allowed the words to revert to their original form. The history may remain unclear, but the song which was eventually produced is unquestionably inspired. It referred to the Battle of Bannockburn of 1314—except for the last two verses which clearly referred to the present:

> By Oppression's woes and pains!
> By your Sons in servile chains!
> We will drain our dearest vains,
>   But they *shall* be free!
>
> Lay the proud Usurpers low!
> Tyrants fall in every foe!
> LIBERTY's in every blow!
>   Let us DO—OR DIE!!!

The Murray Arms takes the credit for housing the poet when he felt inspired to create this rousing anthem. Perhaps they can do a better job now at the Murray Arms of drying wet boots. After all, they've been at it since the hotel was established in 1642. Enlarged and rebuilt in 1760, the Murray Arms at Gatehouse-of-Fleet ought to be a worthwhile stop near the end of a Burns pilgrimage.

Chronologically, the Burns Heritage Trail begins at Alloway in Ayrshire where Burns was born on 25 January 1759. Alloway might have remained unnoticed were it not for Burns. The cottage in which he was born has been restored to admit throngs to one of the most visited houses in Scotland. Nearby is the Alloway Kirk ruin and the picturesque old Brig o'Doon over the River Doon. Years later, he wrote the largely autobiographical *Cotter's Saturday Night* which relates to his early family life in this area:

> The toil-worn Cotter frae his labour goes,
>   This night his weekly moil is at an end,
> Collects his spades, his mattocks and his hoes,
>   Hoping the morn in ease and rest to spend,
> And weary, o'er the muir, his course does hameward bend.

The trail continues. His father, in the struggle to obtain a living as a farmer, left Alloway for the more remote Mount Oliphant farm, a few miles off, where Robert lived until his twelfth year. He was sent to Kirkoswald to learn 'mensuration, surveying and dialling' in the hope that he could be spared the hardships of a farming life. In Kirkoswald, he bragged, he learned to drink (an activity for which he is famous). He also met and fell in love with a young lady (another of his famous activities) who distracted him from trigonometry. His studies were unsuccessful, but he did meet many colourful Kirkoswald people, on whom he later based the characters who appear in his well-known *Tam O'Shanter*. Also on the pilgrim's trail is the thatched cottage of Souter Johnnie, Tam's drinking companion in the poem. The Tam O'Shanter Inn, a favourite alehouse of Burns on his frequent visits to Ayr, appears in that famous work of his and exists today as a museum.

Unremitting poverty followed the family, and another move was made in 1777 to Lochlie, two miles from the village of Tarbolton. To enliven village life, Burns and his friends founded a debating society in 1780, the Bachelors' Club, in a thatched cottage which now serves as a museum.

When his father, worn out by work and worry, died in 1784, the family moved to the neighbouring Mossgiel farm. It still stands, but the best remembrance of the Burns connection there is the poem that he was inspired to write while ploughing, *To a Mountain-Daisy:*

[237]

Wee, modest, crimson-tipped flow'r,
Thou's met me in an evil hour;
For I maun crush amang the stours
  Thy slender stem:
To spare thee now is past my pow'r,
  Thou bonnie gem.

In the nearby village of Mauchline (with its memorial tower that contains yet another museum), he met and fell in love with Jean Armour. The young couple began married life in 1788 in a house in Castle Street, now a museum known, inevitably, as the Burns House. Another Mauchline landmark is Poosie Nansie's Tavern, not much changed from the poet's time and immortalised in *The Jolly Beggars*.

After a final unproductive and unprofitable attempt at farming in Ellisland, Burns became an excise officer and went with his family to Dumfries in 1791. There he spent his final years. At the Globe Inn in Dumfries, the visitor may still imbibe refreshment as Burns did. The family lived in a three-room flat in Wee Vennel (now Bank Street) before moving to a house in Mill Vennell (now Burns Street) where he died on 21 July 1796. That fine sandstone house of two storeys completes the cycle—as you might have guessed—as a museum of Burns relics.

The tourist interested in seeing Scotland would probably unavoidably come upon taverns and sights related to Burns. With luck, a visitor might even chance upon the Murray Arms Hotel. But why take the risk of missing this attractive, old, former coaching inn? It's a place full of character, a friendly place for enjoying a pint with the locals in one of the two cosy bars or for relaxing in one of the four comfortable lounges. With twenty bedrooms, including some rooms in the annexe across the road, the Murray Arms is an ideal location for exploring the historically rich and beautiful countryside.

'A very popular base from which to explore Galloway,' states the hotel brochure. There would seem to be no escape from Burns, for that is exactly what Burns was doing when he stopped at the Murray Arms in Gatehouse-of-Fleet—exploring Galloway. Properly fortified, like Burns, the guest might, like Burns, find poetic inspiration.

★ ★ ★

Robert Louis Stevenson

★ ★ ★
---

at

THE HAWES INN
SOUTH QUEENSFERRY
LOTHIAN
SCOTLAND

> The old Hawes Inn at the Queen's Ferry makes
> a similar call upon my fancy. There it stands,
> apart from the town, beside the pier, in a
> climate of its own, half inland, half marine—
> in front, the ferry bubbling with the tide . . .
> behind, the old garden with the trees.

A Gossip on Romance

Eight miles from Stevenson's birthplace of Edinburgh, on the Firth of Forth where the longest suspension bridge in Britain was completed in 1964, is Queensferry. For some eight hundred years before the gigantic bridge was built, travellers were taken across the Firth of Forth by ferry. In the late eleventh century, Queen Margaret was a regular passenger, thereby giving the town its name.

Just south of the Forth Bridge, an ancient and inconspicuous little inn which has managed to retain its character for some three hundred years, makes itself known because of its literary connections—the Hawes Inn. Sir Walter Scott used the Hawes Inn in *The Antiquary,* and Robert Louis Stevenson took himself and the hero of *Kidnapped* to the inn. Apart from the imposing steel bridge which overhangs the inn today, the scene is very much as it was when Stevenson described it. The ancient-looking grey town straggles westward from the Hawes along a single street, melancholy and sleepy. David Balfour says in Chapter XXVII of *Kidnapped:* 'I was in the long street of Queensferry

R L Stevenson
(1850–1894)
and Hawes Inn,
where both the
author and the
hero of
Kidnapped
stayed

before the sun was up. It was a fairly built burgh, the houses of good stone, many slated; the town-hall not so fine, I thought, as that of Peebles, nor yet the street so noble; but, take it altogether, it put me to shame for my foul tatters.'

The Hawes Inn today is full of charm, with its old oak beams, and is fully capable of transporting the visitor to the past and to the pages of Stevenson's adventure story.

At the Hawes Inn they may kindly point out the room in which the author wrote *Kidnapped* but he actually wrote it many years later while living at Bournemouth. Stevenson is associated with a wide variety of geographical names throughout the world. Because of poor health, and the concomitant need to reside in more salubrious climes than Edinburgh, he developed an early love for travel.

From the time of his birth on 13 November 1850, Robert Louis Stevenson was always frail and sickly. Even as a child, he went to Scottish health resorts or left the cold North altogether for recuperative holidays. His precarious state of health instilled in him a restlessness and made him an incurable wanderer who always collected the memories of places he had been to and enjoyed. Those scenes he stored away to be withdrawn and used as needed in his later writing, making them come alive for future generations.

He had always been a great story-teller with an active imagination. Alison Cunningham, the nurse who looked after him through illnesses and helped to guard his feeble strength, maintained that he was only three when he told her a story he had made up and asked her to write it down. Even if her testimony lacks real evidence, he did dictate to his mother, when he was six, an essay which still exists. By the time he was thirteen, he had written many stories.

He was expected to follow in his father's footsteps and become an engineer. But he desperately wanted to be a writer. He and his father reached an impasse when he found engineering unsuitable as a profession, and his father found writing unacceptable as a career. A compromise was reached when he was allowed to read for the bar. Although he passed the examination and became a lawyer in Edinburgh, he never gave up the idea of authorship. Added to the constant struggle with ill health was the struggle for recognition as a writer.

Fortunately, the places he visited made keen impressions on his mind and gave him sources for his writing. His first book, *An Inland Voyage*, was an account of a canoe trip taken in 1876 in Belgium and France. In it he wrote: 'On my tomb, if ever I have one, I mean to get these words inscribed: "He clung to his paddle".' He did cling to his paddle—that is, to his pen. Two years later he set out on a donkey and described that journey in *Travels with a Donkey in the Cévennes*.

While travelling in France he met Fanny van de Grift Osbourne and made what would seem a most unsuitable match. She was an American, estranged from her husband, with two children (her youngest had recently died), and ten years older than he. Naturally, his parents disapproved and cut off financial support. Fanny returned to California in 1878, and he joined her the following year when he learned that she was suffering from inflammation of the brain. The journey, made in dire circumstances across the ocean on an emigrant ship and then across the country by train, made him critically ill. On arrival, it was he, not Fanny, who was close to death. She nursed him back to health and, her divorce granted, they were married in May 1880.

The strange honeymoon, which included Fanny's twelve-year-old son Lloyd, produced *The Silverado Squatters*. It describes the time spent in a deserted mining camp fifty miles north of San Francisco and makes Silverado sound exotic with depictions of adventure, freedom, excitement. But the author also describes accurately the filth, squalor, discomforts, hardships and dangers of their derelict living quarters in a place infested with rattlesnakes.

On a reconciliation visit to his forgiving and affectionate parents in Edinburgh, Fanny captivated her in-laws and was completely accepted by them. But Stevenson was prevented from living in Scotland by the severe winters which were detrimental to health.

For amusement on one rainy holiday morning in Scotland, young Lloyd drew a map of an imaginary island. His step-father elaborated on the map, labelled it 'Treasure Island' and improvised an accompanying story; thus began Stevenson's first novel, a spontaneous work of fiction with a magic that continues to enchant readers. When it was published as a book in November 1884, *Treasure Island* established his literary reputation.

It was while abroad, during a winter in Davos, that he wrote *A Gossip on Romance* to define his aims in the writing of fiction. After more travelling in the south of France and more serious illness, the Stevensons settled in Bournemouth in a house called Skerryvore. There, as part of his prolific output and proof of versatility, he finished *A Child's Garden of Verses*. He wrote the hugely successful *Dr Jekyll and Mr Hyde*, and he produced, in 1886, *Kidnapped*, the book considered his best by many, including Henry James who came often to Skerryvore to visit his friend. Now, at the age of thirty-six, his financial independence was achieved.

Letters from Bournemouth to his father and to a cousin show how meticulous he was about getting the geography and topography of *Kidnapped* right. He knew the island of Earraid on which the ship is wrecked, and he knew the country in which the young hero wanders and meets Alan Breck. And he certainly knew the Hawes Inn and the 'neighbourhood of the inn.' From the Hawes Inn, David Balfour sets out at the beginning of *Kidnapped*. To it he returns after his dangerous wanderings through the wilderness of Scotland.

So the visitor to Queensferry and the Hawes Inn may actually *feel* the presence there of Robert Louis Stevenson. Identification with the author's words is made complete by looking at the Firth of Forth setting and thinking that:

> . . . backed against a pretty garden of holly-trees and hawthorne, I could see the building which they called the Hawes Inn.

The town of Queensferry lies farther west, and the neighbourhood of the inn looked pretty lonely at that time of day, for the boat had just gone north with passengers.

A year after *Kidnapped* was published, Stevenson, who had remained an invalid during the three-year period spent in Bournemouth, decided to return to America, having been advised to live in Colorado for his health. But the idea of a yacht voyage took hold of him, and he undertook a cruise from San Francisco of the South Pacific.

His wanderings came to an end in Samoa, where he settled in December 1889 and lived for the rest of his life. In Samoa, he wrote *Catriona*, a sequel to *Kidnapped*. He found health and a high literary position in his Utopia.

His sudden death occurred on 3 December 1894 when he was forty-four. He was buried in Samoa, and his own lines are engraved on the tombstone:

> Under the wide and starry sky,
> Dig the grave and let me lie.
> Glad did I live and gladly die,
>   And I laid me down with a will.
>
> This be the verse you grave for me:
> *Here he lies where he longed to be;*
> *Home is the sailor, home from the sea,*
>   *And the hunter home from the hill.*

INDEX